I0549483

Crack the Spine
Spring 2014

Edited by Kerri Farrell Foley

This anthology is generously sponsored by Outskirts Press

Collection Copyright © 2014 Crack the Spine Press, LLC.

Individual works are the sole property of the authors.

ISBN-10: 0988978261
ISBN-13: 978-0-9889782-6-3

Library of Congress Control Number 2014905663

Published by Crack the Spine Press, LLC.
Printed in the United States of America.

Publisher's Note:
This book is a work of fiction. Names, characters, places and incidents are either the product of the author's imagination or are used fictitiously. Any resemblance to actual persons, living or dead, business establishments, events, or locales is entirely coincidental. No part of this book may be reproduced in any manner without the express written consent of the author and/or publisher.

Crack the Spine Press, LLC
Houston, Texas
Hattiesburg, Mississippi
www.crackthespinepress.com

CONTENTS

Off the Curb

It was a windy June day, and clumps of clouds churned across the sky as Gwendolyn stepped out of Gleason's Fish with halibut for dinner. She glanced upward, the leaves on the trees hassled into a shimmying frenzy, and she failed to recognize that she had dawdled to a halt in the middle of the street until the honking horn of a Range Rover reminded her.

Gwendolyn hopped up onto the curb and proceeded down the hill to her car, which was parked in the town center of Merrimac-on-the-Hudson. As she rummaged in her purse for her keys, a particularly virulent gust of wind clamped her skirt to her thighs, and in that moment she saw, in the heart shaped leaves of a linden tree, what appeared to be a myriad of tiny, clenched fists, or were they faces? There were dozens of them, hundreds, the entire tree crawling with otherworldly life.

No. This is not real.

Clutching her handbag, Gwendolyn leaned against the sun-baked enamel of her Pepper White Mini Cooper. The clear coat, she whispered—the words a kind of mantra—would offer scratch-resistant protection. Microscopic ceramic particles in the paint, the dealer had explained, hardened in the shop oven for a forty percent improvement in paint gloss compared to traditional clear coats. She clicked open the door with sweaty palms.

A short time later, her nerves steadied by the drive home, Gwendolyn was putting broccoli on to steam when the back door slammed, and Gus entered the kitchen, lacrosse stick in hand.

"Perfect timing," Gwendolyn said. "Do you want to change and we'll eat?"

"I'll be right down," Gus said, heading into the hallway and taking the stairs two at a time.

"And tell Bram dinner's ready," she called after him.

"I'm here," Bram said, appearing in the doorway. He was sixteen and as tall as his older brother, but more slender, with fine, straight brown hair like Gwendolyn.

"Could you help set the table?" she asked. "I was thinking maybe inside tonight. It looks like rain."

"It isn't raining," Bram said. "It's just windy."

Gwendolyn shrugged as Bram carried napkins and utensils out to the patio. Wide brick steps led down to the lawn, and the sun had dipped behind the cedars, the basin of day full to overflowing, puddles of light spilling over the table as they ate. No matter how precipitously the branches bowed in the wind, though, Gwendolyn resisted the temptation to look at them. Instead she watched her children's faces, tethered by the sound of their voices.

~~~

A little past nine that evening, Gwendolyn was emptying the dishwasher when Frank came home, dropped his briefcase by the front door and walked down the hallway.

"Another late night," she said.

"The client called at five o'clock with changes that he wanted for tomorrow. What a jerk." He shook his head and opened the refrigerator. Pulling out his plate, he peered at the fogged over plastic.

"What's this?"

"Halibut."

"Looks good. Thanks, hon." He slid the plate into the microwave and spread the New York Times on the counter.

"How are the boys?" he asked, glancing over the front page. "Is Bram ready for his chemistry final?"

"I think so. Why don't you go say hi when you're done."

"I will. Everything else alright?"

Gwendolyn watched as he ate, his gaze skimming an article, and she decided to wait to see how long it would take for him to notice that she hadn't answered. In his khakis and button down shirt, his feet bare with a tuft of dark hair on each toe, he reminded Gwendolyn of a satyr dressed as a man, or a hobbit, better suited to padding swiftly over the forest floor.

"Gwendolyn? How was your day?"

"It was . . . fine."

He turned back to the paper.

~~~

The following afternoon Gwendolyn was outside painting lanterns of different shapes and sizes for the party planning business that she had started when Frank had been out of work. She held her breath, spray-painted a batch, and then stepped back to let the aerosol cloud of white settle. After a few rounds she turned to discover Bram watching her.

"What are you doing?" he asked, his shoulder weighted down by his backpack.

"Making magic," she grinned. "It's for the Lindzer wedding."

"Looks like a lot of work."

"Imagine what I'd do if I had a daughter. Not that I won't help you with your wedding. If you want."

"I have no plans to get married any time soon, mom."

"Well that's a good thing, Bram, because I kind-of have my hands full right now anyway." Bram smiled, and as Gwendolyn watched him go, a tiny fissure tore beneath her ribcage, the fine white thread of a scar, crows' feet on the surface of her heart. In two months Gus would leave for college, and a year later, Bram. She absentmindedly shook the can of spray paint and glanced over at the plum tree, its burgundy leaves infused with the sun's rays. As she watched, the variegated light within the tree morphed with surprising rapidity, becoming almost gelatinous, with a pinkish, oily sheen as the spaces between the leaves resolved themselves into clusters of mobile, jabbering faces. Catching her breath, the paint can fell to Gwendolyn's side. Tentatively, she took a step towards the diminutive faces, their voices crackling like plastic wrappers.

She peered at the tiny noses and ears on their hairless heads, the creatures' expressions fluctuating quickly, at turns querulous or fierce, astonished or mirthful. Inching nearer, she tried to detect the color of

3

their deep set eyes, or whether or not they had any teeth, but when she was still ten feet away the faces froze, and the staticky sound of their talking ceased.

"Who are you?" Gwendolyn whispered. She glanced towards the house, worried that Bram might hear, but neither his room nor the kitchen was within earshot.

"I won't hurt you," she continued, her own voice sounding foolish to her ears. "Are you real? Or am I crazy?" A tinkling, like bells. Laughter?

"Who else can see you? Are you everywhere, in every tree, or are you a kind of spirit that inhabits different trees at different times?" The faces were dancing, now, quivering, the sound like wind through dried leaves, unlike any language she could discern but so loud that Gwendolyn looked up and down the street, certain that someone would hear and come out of their house to see what the commotion was, but the sidewalks remained empty, each house set back from the road on a half acre lot. She took another step towards the branches. The faces were the size of large crabapples, and squished as they were, it was difficult to distinguish their features, but when she was still four or five feet away their movements fizzled, then evaporated completely.

"Wait!" Gwendolyn cried. "Come back . . . *please?*"

"Mom? Mom!"

"What, Bram?" she yelled in the direction of the house.

"When will dinner be ready?"

Gwendolyn glanced at her unfinished work. "I'm coming in now!" She turned back to the tree, but all she saw was leaves, and with a flush of annoyance she dragged her tarp back into the garage and hurried inside.

~~~

That Saturday, Frank and Gwendolyn were transplanting one of the Japanese maple saplings that sprouted each year beneath the tree in the corner of the back yard.

4

"Look at the leaves," Frank said as he laid a green slip on his palm. "They have five digits, just like us." Gwendolyn laughed and glanced at him curiously.

"Maybe they talk to each other," she said.

Frank bent down to loosen the sapling. Together they lifted it from the ground and carried it to the front yard.

"I think she'll like it here," Gwendolyn said as she poured mulch around the base of the seedling.

"Yeah, it looks good," Frank said, perusing their yard.

They had moved into the house when Gus and Bram were toddlers, having no idea that it would take twelve years to save up enough money to replace the drafty windows and the outdated electrical system. The renovation had been almost complete when the economy had collapsed, and Frank had spent the next eight months out of work. When he had finally found a job at a boutique firm in the city, his salary a fraction of what it had been, and with a boss nearly half his age, Frank had considered himself lucky. The financial uncertainty, though, had given Gwendolyn the push she had needed to start her party planning business, and luckily there were apparently still people in and around Merrimac with enough money to pay for their children's weddings or their own retirement parties.

"Alright," Frank said, wiping his brow. "Are you happy with your tree?"

"Yes I am. What shall we call her? Betsy, Lucretia?"

Frank snorted. "How about Plant?"

"You're just pretending to be a grouch," Gwendolyn said, putting her arm around him. "Besides, why is it my tree? You always make it seem as though the yard has nothing to do with you."

"Is that why I'm out here right now? What I like is doing something with you."

Gwendolyn squeezed his shoulder, feeling the solid weight of him. At fifty, Frank was still in great shape.

"If Gus and I are going to go to the gym before dinner, though, I'd better get going," Frank said.

5

"Is Bram going too?"

"Sure, yeah." Gwendolyn noticed his slight hesitation, but it wasn't, she thought, that Frank favored Gus, not exactly. It was more that he simply found it easier to be with Gus. The two of them talked about sports and played fantasy football together, whereas Bram was more interested in obscure, complicated technology that Gwendolyn, also, had a hard time following. Maybe, she thought, when Gus was away at college it would give Bram and his father a chance to spend a little more time together.

"Do you want to help water the tree before you go?" she asked.

Frank glanced at his watch, and she felt his gesture like a drop in barometric pressure; in a minute he would be gone.

"Something strange happened to me this week," she said in a rush.

"What do you mean?"

"I know this sounds ridiculous, but I think maybe I was hallucinating."

"What?" He laughed. "Magic lanterns, trees with names; you weren't hallucinating, honey. You just need to get out of the house more."

"Excuse me?"

"I didn't mean that. You know I didn't mean that. Gwen —" She hated it when he called her Gwen, a name he only used when he was trying to placate her.

"We had a nice afternoon," he said. "Do you want to ruin everything because of one thoughtless comment?" He stared at her with his slate blue eyes, his dark hair speckled with gray; her handsome husband.

"I don't want to ruin anything, Frank." She kneeled down and scooped the mulch into a ring around the trunk, creating a basin to hold the water. "And you're right," she said carefully. "If you want to get back in time for dinner, you'd better go." She stood, her expression neutral, a smooth surface for him to slip away on.

After Frank and Gus had left, Gwendolyn stopped by the plum tree beside the garage. It was a windless day, the russet leaves tranquil in the afternoon light. She stared at the branches, willing the faces to appear, but the leaves remained still.

What's going to happen, she whispered, *when Gus and Bram leave, and it's just Frank and me?* She closed her eyes, then opened them again.

As she walked away the light, in her periphery, liquefied, becoming viscous and thick. Gwendolyn whipped around as the faces, once again, filled the tree. They were everywhere, like a hive seething with honeybees, each face perfectly formed and distinct and yet part of a larger whole. The energy they emitted was overwhelming. Impulsively she ran towards them, reaching out her hand to touch their skin or feel the imprint of their tiny teeth around her finger.

As soon as she was within grasp, though, the faces melted away. Gwendolyn brushed her hand over the bark, but no residue remained.

~~~

She found herself checking the tree several times a day. She couldn't figure out a pattern to the faces' appearance, but if more than twenty-four hours went by without their materializing she became distracted, finding it difficult to focus on her work. One rainy Monday, after not having seen them all weekend, she trekked in and out of the house every few hours, a band tightening around her heart each time she found the leaves glistening but unchanged. Finally the next morning, loaded down with groceries, Gwendolyn glanced up and the faces were there. She didn't dare set down her bags as she stood enthralled, the dips and lulls of the creatures' babble filling her with bemusement, but with something else as well, something almost like joy. When eventually they vanished, Gwendolyn continued into the house, and as she stacked the peanut butter in the cabinet and organized the milk in the refrigerator her sense of well-being lingered, as if her connection to a world vast and wonderful, a source of limitless possibility, remained. Gnawing at the edge of her consciousness, though, was the fear that inevitably this grace would fade, and when it did, she would be left feeling even more stripped and bare than before.

~~~

7

A few evenings later, after the dinner dishes were washed and Bram and Gus had left the table, Gwendolyn slipped on her shoes and went outside. The backyard was shrouded in shadow. It was early July, the evenings warm as she turned on the faucet at the side of the house. She picked up the hose as a sudden movement made her turn to see a hummingbird, its wings a blur, dart over to the lilac tree and then zip away.

"Maybe you weren't real, either," Gwendolyn muttered. She started to spray the planters on the patio when a loud rustling made her look up to see Bram approaching from around the side of the house.

"Oh!" she said. "You surprised me."

"It's Tuesday. I brought down the garbage."

"Thanks for remembering. Guess what I just saw—a hummingbird."

"Is that who you were talking to?"

"Not exactly. I was more talking to myself."

"I talk to myself a lot," Bram said.

"Do you? I've never heard you."

"It wouldn't be talking to myself if you were there."

Gwendolyn chuckled. "Good point." Giving the hose a tug, she pulled it over to the vegetable garden.

"Whoa," Bram said, looking upwards. "What are those? Are they bats?"

Gwendolyn turned to where he was pointing as a series of small, dark forms darted across a navy sky. "I think they are."

"That's crazy. Why haven't I seen them before?"

"Maybe you needed to be out here at just this time, when it's dark enough for the bats to come out, but still light enough to see." They stood for a moment, gazing upward.

"Did you know that a moth's sense of smell is so acute that it can detect individual molecules?" Bram asked. "And birds can see colors over four wavelengths of light compared to human retinas, which can only detect three?"

"I didn't know that," Gwendolyn said. She was tempted to reach over and brush Bram's bangs from his forehead as she might have done when he was small, but she turned on the hose instead, so the words—*when you are gone, I will no longer know your thoughts in my every day*—would stay inside her.

Bram went inside, and Gwendolyn soon followed. She used to enjoy lingering in the yard, watching the light drain from the sky, but recently, just being outside put her on edge. If she turned her head too quickly or blinked in the sun, she might think she saw the faces fading in or out in a distant tree, but the only place she actually saw them, after that first incident in town, was the plum tree. With every day that passed she became more anxious and irritable. She snapped at Gus for leaving his lacrosse stick in the hallway, and at Frank for not putting away his clothes, simple, everyday tasks becoming shabby and dull until eventually, like a long awaited rain, the leaves would start to tremble. The air would thicken, becoming mercurial and alive, and the tiny beings would emerge once again.

As July tipped into August, though, and heat settled over the earth like a balm, the spaces between appearances grew longer. Soon several weeks had gone by without a visitation, until one day Gwendolyn found herself staring at a cookbook that she had left open on the counter, unable to make sense of the squiggly black lines of a recipe that she had made many times before. In an attempt to clear her head she gathered her cutting shears and went outside to pick a bouquet of Knockout roses and Stella de Oro daylilies from her garden. As she reached through the prickly branches, though, she was dismayed to see the leaves riddled with the rusty holes left by Japanese beetles, clumps of crabgrass blooming over the mulch. Her garden had always been a place of refuge, but even here, she thought with despair, her world had become tawdry and frayed.

~~~

She was emptying the dishwasher when Frank came home. He opened the refrigerator and peered through the plastic wrap covering his dinner.

9

"Is this chicken?" he asked. "Looks great. Is it a new recipe?"

"No, Frankie. It's not a new recipe."

"What's in it?"

"Chicken."

Frank glanced at her. "Are you alright?"

"I'm fine. How are you?"

"You seem kind of cranky."

Gwendolyn placed the last glass in the cabinet. "I'm just tired."

When Frank opened the paper, Gwendolyn walked down the hallway. She glanced back to where Frank stood illuminated in the kitchen doorway before opening the front door and slipping outside. The dew-damp lawn was cool against her bare feet, blades of grass sticking between her toes, and fireflies glowed like the neon pegs of the Light Bright toy that Gus and Bram had played with as children.

Banks of shadows loomed where trees had stood by day, the branches of the plum tree shining silver in the light of the rising moon. Gwendolyn paused, taking in this nighttime transformation. Where did the faces go, she wondered, when they were not here, and what would happen in the winter, when there were no leaves? Were they like cherry blossoms, erupting into bloom only to scatter like snow? It had been three weeks since Gwendolyn had seen the faces, and they were an ache inside, a constant, hollow burn.

Why would you come, she whispered, *only to go away?*

Gwendolyn approached the tree and reached through the branches as twigs scratched her face. Her heart beat rapidly, as if, she thought, she was violating a sacred space, but she didn't care. For weeks she had waited, hoping and willing the faces to come, but they hadn't, and Gwendolyn feared that they were gone forever. Pressing her forehead against the bark, she squeezed shut her eyes.

I'm going to stay here all night, she whispered. *I'm going to stay until Frankie discovers that I'm gone, and when he comes to look for me, I'm going to hide in the tree, and he won't see me in the dark. He'll call me, and Gus and Bram will come out, and they won't see me either. I'll dissolve, just like the faces, until all*

10

that will be left will be an iridescent smudge, and the faces will take me with them, and I will be gone.

The house, though, remained still. No one came to look for her, and mosquitoes started to buzz in her ear. Gwendolyn tried to see the time, but she couldn't make out the hands of her watch in the dark.

Sliding her arms down the bark, almost hoping the scratches would draw blood, she pulled herself back and turned towards the house. When she opened the door Frank was no longer haloed in the kitchen doorway. She heard Gus's electronic music playing too loudly from upstairs, and she continued into the bedroom. As she switched on the light she saw Frank sitting on the bed.

"Frankie?"

"Where were you?" he asked. "I looked for you in your study."

"I was outside."

"What were you doing?"

"I visited the plum tree."

"Gwendolyn?" Caught within the cadence of his voice she heard something halting and unsure.

"I see faces," she said. "They come and go, and I haven't seen them for a long time, and I miss them." She started to cry, softly at first, then tears streaming down her cheeks. Frank patted the bed beside him and she sat down.

"You tried to tell me, didn't you?" he said. "And I didn't listen."

Tears fell off her chin, and she watched them land, dark splatters on her jeans.

"I'm listening now, though," Frank said gently. When she didn't answer, he put his arm around her. "It's going to be okay."

"No it's not," she stammered. "Nothing is okay. Everything is falling apart, and I don't know what to do or where it's all gone."

"Oh Gwendolyn. Nothing is falling apart. You have me, and the boys, and we love you."

"But they're going away, Frankie. They're leaving us, first Gus, then Bram, and then what?"

11

"Gus and Bram aren't going away forever. They're only going to college. And what am I, chopped liver?" He drew back to look at her, and she could see the skin slack around his eyes, and she smiled because she knew that she looked worse.

"I need a tissue."

He reached for one on the bedside table, and when he wiped her cheek she put her hand over his. For just a moment she wondered what would happen if she held on and didn't let go.

The Mind-House

My mind-house
is a dimlit echo chamber,
where choked gaslamp hallways
find bright, empty rooms.
A maze
where I take my after dinner walks,
touring all the strange exhibits.

My mind-house
employs a staff,
scuttering unnoticed,
they polish through the night.
A smirking butler
who greets the guests,
ushered through
my swinging doors.

My mind-house has
a front porch
where I take my morning tea,
peering out behind dewy eyes.
A staircase
built with many books,
the last steps fraught
with point-blank pages.

My mind-house
has a kitchen,
you'll find me nibbling

at fermented memory.
The surplus pantry,
over-engineered
hunger hoard,
beyond all inventory.

My mind-house
has no foundation,
a work of earth,
instinct's inception.
My mind-house
is a haunted cage
possessed by
the mind in question.

The Birds of Bristol Court

FLORA

The widow Florrine Smythe, who preferred to be called Flora, but not Flo, lived at 16 Bristol Court.

Flora sat on the stool in front of her dressing table, feeling her bottom spill over just a little on the sides. Once she had finished her facial work, she would carefully squeeze herself into her foundation garment, which worked in a ruthless and primitive way by pushing a lot of her upward in a flattering way. The problem was that when she had it on, she could barely breathe and was forced to sit only on the edge of the furniture. Three hours was about all she could take. She knew that the proper solution was to lose fifteen pounds, and every time she put the damn thing on, she committed to do just that, but soon after she had it off, and mealtime or between-meal time arrived, her resolve melted in the face of temptation.

MILDRED

The young widow, Mildred Forsythe, lived next door at 18 Bristol Court in a house that, at first glance, looked the same but, on closer examination, was just a little finer than Flora's in every tasteful detail.

Mildred, who was seldom called Millie, was seated in her living room, trying to stay focused on a needlepoint pillow cover. Every few minutes, she walked to the front window, parted the drapes a fraction of an inch, and looked out onto the street.

On her fifteenth trip, her vigil was rewarded. A car pulled into Flora's driveway and disappeared as the garage door was raised and lowered to allow the car to slip into the vacant spot in Flora's two-car garage. Mildred knew the car, having seen this performance many times before. It belonged to Lucia Fiorini, one of the kitchen staff at the country club, who was delivering another meal that Flora would heat up and pass off as her own, with much theatrical detail. Mildred told her friend Betty that Flora would have made the perfect television chef, if only she knew how to cook.

Mildred now knew with certainty that right around six o'clock she would see Harold Overmeyer emerge from his house, dressed for an evening at Flora's. Harry would have been invited for 6:00 p.m. He would never be unfashionably early, but he would also not dare to be late.

HARRY

Harold Overmeyer, a widower, lived at 17 Bristol Court, almost directly across the street from Flora and Mildred, indifferent to the subtle differences between the widows' houses.

Harry was watching the Giants-Steelers game, which had gone into overtime. He looked at his watch. He was due at Flora's in twenty minutes for cocktails, and he could not be late. He knew from experience he would not get his second drink if he were late. She would rush him right to dinner, thereby upsetting the flow of his entire evening. An evening with Flora required at least two manhattans. He felt so awkward around intelligent women. He wished Joan were there to steady him, which was absurd: the only reason he was with this woman was because Joan was gone.

He was going to miss the tense sudden-death ending. He still had to shower, shave, and dress. He amended the budgeted time for his toilet to ten minutes, down from fifteen. He wished he had listened more carefully to his son Jeffery, who had shown him how to record a program in progress. He looked at the remote, which had over fifty little buttons. He hesitated and then, afraid if he pushed the wrong button the whole system would self-destruct, gave up, sighed, pushed "Off," and headed for the shower.

At 6:01 p.m., Harry, combing the few hairs left on his head as he walked, hurried across the street. He glanced up at Mildred's front window but did not see her because, except for one eyeball, she was concealed behind closed drapery.

16

DINNER

Flora was stiffly perched on the edge of the sofa, trying to breathe more or less naturally. Harry was deep in the wing chair, which must have been the favorite of her late husband, Charles, whose portraits at every stage of advancing age and weight were scattered around the house.

"Shall we eat?" said Flora brightly.

"Sure, Flora," said Harry, smiling, "but let's have just one more short one."

Flora left Harry to make the drinks while she went to the kitchen to pretend to put the finishing touches on the meal.

She stirred and tasted, wondering how she could get Harry off the subject of his grandson Zeke. "A good kick in the pants—that's what he needs," Harry had said at least three times, and she knew the repetition would increase with the second manhattan. He never had more than two, and then a glass of wine or two. She could live with that. At the right level of alcohol, he was a delight, but it was a narrow band.

Harry joined her in the kitchen, handed her a fresh drink, and walked to the window. "Had a terrible drive today on that hole," he said, pointing across the cart path to the golf course. "Sliced it over the rough; ended up somewhere over here, I think, in Mildred's bushes. Out of bounds—a new four-dollar Titleist."

Flora, coming to his side, could not imagine a more boring subject than golf. "It doesn't look that bad, do you think?" she said. "Can you imagine that thing could cause such a stink?"

Harry looked out the window again. He couldn't imagine what she was talking about. "I'm sorry, Flora, you lost me. What thing?"

She pointed. "My bird feeder—right there." There was Flora's bird feeder, ten feet away, with a squirrel sitting on it, greedily spilling sunflower seeds. Until the day before, he hadn't even known it existed, even though he drove past it every day in his golf cart. No one could see it, except from Flora's kitchen.

"Charlie's sister gave it to me. Usually, I forget to fill it, but now I'll be damned if I'll take it down. I won't stand by and let that bitch Alice try to push her weight around. She thinks she's queen of the condos."

The damn thing had nearly caused them to be late for their tee time. When he dropped by to pick up his golf buddy Simon Morgan, Simon's wife Alice had made Harry sign a petition in support of her campaign to force the removal of Flora's birdhouse. "I signed the petition to allow it to remain," said Harry, which was true because, as it happened, later that same day Martha Birnbaum had arrived with a petition to allow the feeder to stay. Martha loved to talk. Without hesitation, he signed it and encouraged her to move on to get more signatures.

"You're a doll," said Flora.

Flora went back to the stove for some more culinary stage business. He walked over and stood very close to her at the stove. He leaned against her, then glanced down at her slimmed, solidified hips and waist, puzzled by what was different about them. She rattled the cover on the empty saucepan prop she had placed on the stove top, then added a touch of pepper to the mysterious mixture of ingredients on the stove and, finally, fiddled with the controls, turning one up and then back down again. "There," she said. "Just needed to kick it up a little."

Dinner went smoothly, although she never got Harry too far from the subject of his lazy 25-year-old grandson. Then Harry insisted on helping her clean up. "You spent hours in the kitchen. It's the least I could do," he said.

She appreciated the gesture, but she was dying to release her confined body from its straitjacket and snuggle onto the couch. Cleanup could wait until morning, and she was sick of Zeke. So she said she had a headache.

Harry put his arm around her and held her close. "My fault," he said. "I talk too much." Ten minutes later, he left.

As soon as the door closed behind Harry, she slipped her dress off, unhooked all the stays, unzipped all the zippers on her girdle/corset/bustier, stepped out of it and, almost naked, feeling giddy

18

and almost weightless, danced a few steps around the room. She flopped into Charlie's armchair, where Harry had sat. He wasn't perfect, but she had a warm feeling about Harry. Tomorrow, she'd clean up the mess and go shopping for some equally powerful but more comfortable underwear.

Harry walked slowly home. He sat in the dark for a few minutes, then turned on the TV and tuned to a basketball game. He sighed, and although he had no interest in the game, there were too many thoughts in his head to sleep. He leaned back on the sofa and allowed the flickering light from the game to dance around the room. He couldn't decide if she was shallow and superficial or charming and genuine. Somehow she seemed to understand him, know how to please him, make him comfortable.

THE MAIL

The mailboxes for 16, 17, and 18 Bristol Court are mounted together on a single post at the curb on the widows' side of the street. The next morning, at 11:30 a.m., Harry walked across the street to check his mailbox. He saw Mildred emerge from her front door thirty seconds later, with her coat wrapped around her shoulders, but he did not notice the curtains in Flora's front window stir. Mildred walked toward the mailbox with her head down, watching her steps. He waited. "Hello, Mildred."

She looked up and smiled. "Oh," she said, "Harry, I'm frightfully sorry. I guess I didn't see you."

Harry went through his thin pile of mail. "Bills and junk. That's all I get," he said.

Mildred, who didn't seem to have any mail, said, "Did you and Simon Morgan play eighteen yesterday?" Harry nodded. "So he's back from his business trip."

"Got in late—night before," said Harry. "Barely made our tee time."

"That's nice," she said, smiling at him again, brushing a wisp of hair away from her face. "Well, have a nice day. I have to hurry—Monday

19

lecture at the Prosser. I never miss it. So nice to see you, Harry."

"Yeah, it seems like we always meet at the mailbox," he said. Harry, who did not wonder why Mildred seemed so interested in Simon, walked back across the street, set the mail on the hall table, and then went into the den, turned the television on, and started flipping through the channels. He'd never been to a lecture in his life.

After attending the art lecture, Mildred stopped at an antiques shop and then an independent bookstore that served espresso superior to Starbucks'. Back home she gardened in her tiny backyard, prepared a light crepes Véronique for herself, dined alone, cleaned up, then sat in her perfectly decorated and appointed living room and turned on the gas fireplace with the fake logs that burned but were never consumed. She read by the cone of light from the reading lamp next to her chair as darkness overtook the rest of the house.

WHAT FLORA SAW

Fretting about the bird-feeder meeting the next day, it was midnight when Flora turned out the lights and headed to her bedroom. As she glanced out at her bird feeder, out of the corner of her eye she thought she saw a silhouette in the dim light from the security lights along the golf-cart path. The figure stepped carefully into Mildred's yard—a man. Before she could get to the phone and dial 911, he stepped on something and hopped in pain. At the same instant, Mildred's back-porch light flashed on and off, the door opened, Mildred's head appeared, and she more or less pulled the hopping intruder into her house.

Flora lay in bed, the worries about the bird feeder replaced by a replay of the scene of Harry and Mildred chitchatting at the mailbox. Could it be Harry?

THE MEETING

Harry arrived at Flora's dressed in coat and tie, in accordance with the club's dress code. Flora looked different. She looked fabulous. He hadn't realized she had a waist. Usually, she looked sort of lumpy.

Then, last Sunday she had a new shape: better but strange, firm and round, sort of like an ice cream cone. Tonight she had a red silk dress smoothly wrapped around her that showed she had a real figure. She pirouetted for him. "So, what do you think? I bought it at Nordstrom today." He noticed her face was softer, with less harsh color. "They helped me with the makeup too. I think I lost the hang of it."

"You look—you look wonderful." They set off in their finery in Flora's electric cart down the cart path on the third fairway.

The room was packed. Alice Morgan, who served on the condo board, was the instigator and leader of the campaign to remove the bird feeder. In accordance with Alice's interpretation of the rules, the Royce Management Company had told Flora to remove it. Flora had appealed to the board.

They ran into Simon at the door.

"I'm surprised to see you here, Simon," said Flora.

"Oh, I wouldn't miss this," said Simon. "I've got a surprise for you, Harry." He handed Harry a golf ball. "That's your mark, isn't it?"

"Thanks," said Harry. "Where the hell did you find this?"

Simon laughed. "I stepped on it in the dark," said Simon as his wife rapped her gavel and called the meeting to order. Flora glanced at the ball as Harry slipped it in his jacket pocket. It said "Titleist."

Alice explained to the condo owners what they already knew, that they could do as they liked to the interior, but the outside of the houses and all the grounds, landscaping included, even everyone's front yard and backyard, were maintained by a management company engaged by the condominium association. Flora leaned toward Harry and said in a loud whisper, "That's interesting. What about Alice's flower garden?"

The anti-feeder speakers, of which there were many, seized on the concept of "precedent," and all said the same thing in slightly different ways: that is, they had no problem with this particular bird feeder, which was tasteful and even not unattractive, but it would set a precedent, implying that soon Bristol Court would be overwhelmed by ugly bird feeders.

Harry slouched down in his chair wondering how it was possible

21

for time to pass so slowly, when a late arrival caught his attention. She made a stir, because there were hardly any vacant chairs, and several men rose to offer her a seat. Simon Morgan removed his jacket from the empty chair next to him and she sat. Harry looked up and saw that Alice Morgan, sitting at the head table, was glaring at the new arrival who had interrupted the meeting.

As the woman sat, she turned toward Harry and smiled, but he had never seen her before. He'd thought by this time he had seen everyone on Bristol Court, especially the attractive women, of whom there were not many. She was wearing a plain black dress, what Harry called a "cocktail dress." It was simple, with a round neck and long sleeves, but it clung to her slim figure in a fascinating way. Her lips had a hint of color. Her hair was sort of silver; pulled up, exposing her neck. Flora didn't seem to be paying her any attention. She must have known her.

Mona Finnigan pointed out that many birds had come to depend upon the feeder and would starve if it were removed. Martha Birnbaum, the leader of the Flora supporters and a sweet lady, took even longer to point out the number of species that used this area as part of their migratory path, including several species Harry had never heard of, including one called a "tit," which struck Harry as amusing. Finally, someone shouted, "You forgot the blue-footed booby, Martha!" and Martha, the sweet old lady, turned and hissed through clenched teeth, "Who said that?" Armond Zambini quoted from the United States Constitution and stated that things had come to a sorry state when a man could have the right to carry a handgun, when they could all shoot at each other, but were forbidden to feed the poor hungry birds. He had a deep booming voice, and his speech was simultaneously ridiculous and moving.

Suddenly, the door to the meeting room was flung open, and the condo association's attorney rushed to the front of the room in a bustling flurry of paper. He apologized for being late, then announced that the motion under debate was out of order. The birdhouse was "explicitly" banned by the rules. The rules could be changed only by a two-thirds majority vote by petition at the annual meeting, which would take place in approximately eight months. The room erupted into mass confusion. Alice Morgan, sitting at the head table, turned quietly to the chairman, who nodded, struck his gavel, and the board filed out of the room. The meeting was over.

It was now after six. "Well, that's that," said Flora. "Let's go to dinner."

As Flora and Harry stood, the beautiful stranger also stood, turned, and approached them. "Hello, Harry. Hello, Flora," she said.

"Hello, Mildred," said Flora.

Mildred, thought Harry—*another Mildred?*

The woman gave Harry a strange look. "Don't you recognize me? Do I look that bad?"

It was Mildred—his neighbor Mildred. "I'm sorry," he stammered. "The dress. You changed your hair."

"Yes, it is quite a dress, isn't it?" said Flora. "Well, come along, Harry."

Harry didn't budge. "I'm so sorry, Mildred. We're staying at the club for dinner. Are you alone? Why don't you join us?"

Suddenly, Harry felt himself being forcibly yanked toward the door. "I'm sure she has other plans," said Flora.

DINNER AT THE CLUB

At the bar, Flora was greeted warmly by a few of her supporters. The opponents avoided her and would not meet her eye unless Flora spoke to them, which she made a concerted effort to do.

Harry stopped in the men's locker room, where all the talk was about Mildred.

In the ladies' lounge, Flora ran into her chief supporter, Martha Birnbaum.

"So, what did you think of Mildred's dress?" said Martha.

Flora looked around to see who was in earshot. "Alice better watch out," said Flora.

"Alice Morgan?"

"Trust me on this one, Martha," said Flora, raising her eyebrows

23

knowingly.

They left the lounge together. "Uh-oh," said Martha. "Here they come. See you later." Martha left hurriedly as Alice and Simon Morgan approached, arm in arm.

Flora moved behind a potted palm, then stepped out in front of them. "Well, hello, Alice," she said cheerfully.

"Flora," said Alice, "I'm so sorry about the last-minute lawyer thing. It took me totally and completely by surprise, as you can imagine." She took Flora's hand. "I really, personally, have no objection to the feeder, but I'm on the board, you know, and as a board member—"

"Oh, give it a rest, Alice," said Simon.

"Actually, Alice," said Flora, "to tell you the truth, I really don't give a shit one way or the other. By the way," she continued, "don't you think Mildred looked stunning tonight? She is finally coming out of her shell. It's been so hard for her since she lost Desmond." Alice and Simon exchanged a quick glance, but not quick enough for Flora to miss the look of dread on Alice's face. It was a moment Flora would cherish, worth a thousand bird feeders.

Flora drifted through the club dining room, bestowing a relaxed smile on friends and enemies alike, finally arriving at the corner table where Harry was waiting. He smiled. "You were gone so long, I was beginning to worry about you," he said. He stood and held her chair for her. "I hope you are not too distressed, Flora, about the way things went at the meeting."

Flora, unrestrained by her new undergarment, turned gracefully and gave Harry a public and possessive kiss on the cheek. "Harry," she said, "I don't think I've felt so wonderful in years. I'm so glad you got your four-dollar Titleist back." She turned to the young man in the starched white jacket standing next to the table. "Thomas, Mr. Overmeyer will have a Canadian Club manhattan, and I shall have the same—with two cherries." She turned to Harry, reached across the table, and squeezed his hand, the glow of triumph on her face.

24

Daily Life and Other Oddities

MOVIE TICKET

Crumpled crumpling craving of life of social interactions. Entertaining interactions for days, upon days, upon days. Days of new, new never needless, new never needless needling its way into an esophagus.

Esophagus, ectopic, endometriosis, elephants in the eyes of archaic symphonies. Symphonies signifying failing free-floating beings. Beings being belated bodies, behaving badly while barely beating the drum, the drum dumbing daily down the beaten path.

COUPON

Clipping, creasing, caving, caving into treats where we meet, where we meet meat and honey. Honey and sugar. Sugar and milk. Milk milking mayhem outside of a shambled house. Housing carousels and baby laughs. Laughter outside of laughter outside of empathy is no more. More, more, more.

RECEIPT

Ching, ching, ching, of clinging masses to falling houses outside everyday life. Life and strife upon strife upon strife, lifting and crumbling before our very eyes. Eyes set upon lies upon silicone dreams and silicone happiness. Happiness is passing this is passing this trust and lust.

Lusting upon a trusting soul, upon a trusting sole, upon a trusting sole of feet and liver.

PAPER

Daily dos and daily don'ts, did we do the dancing droughts and dipping days of dreary dawns and sets. Sets upon sets, upon rows of sets of fine china and lily pads. Pads of dog feet and pads of pencils, scratching, stroking, shaking across a manila page. A manila page, a lined page, a dark page, a crumpled page. A page of yellowed age and fragrant happiness. Happiness and loneliness, two flips of the same coin, adjoining, coining tones and ambiences.

Species

I am happy all the time. Well, not all the time, I don't suppose someone could possibly be happy all the time. I was not happy when my father passed away. Not because it is respectful to mourn the loss of a loved one but because I chose to feel the sadness. Yes, you should always aim to experience everything once. And there could not be a better time to do so than now, when we are breathing through human bodies and are able to decide what we will and will not do. I find this so-called free choice only humans possess exhilarating. It makes me proud to be part of the human race. It is said – or I have heard somewhere, it must have been on one of those documentaries – that language separates us from all other species. That can't possibly be right. The only way we could make such a statement is if we understood the language of all other species, should they have one of course. I am not arguing that capacities differ among species, hell, I am multi-tasking right now. One part of my brain is currently educating itself on important life issues while the other, more younger part, is present in a department store restaurant, actively engaging in a social conversation with my best friend in the entire world. Well, not the entire world precisely, as I have not met every single person on the planet. Who knows, the lady feeding her baby next to our table might be an even better friend than she is a mother.

But isn't that part of the problem though: the fact that I do not know everybody? If that were the case I would greet every stranger, only they would no longer be strangers. Every face would have a name, goodness, how would I go about remembering all their names? Even the homeless would be connected to me. I promise I would give each of them their daily coins to find a place to sleep. If only I knew everybody. With every siren from a rushing ambulance

I would hold my breath. No longer could I selfishly wish the ambulance wasn't carrying one of my own. I would visit countless funerals to bid my farewell and console those left behind. All breaking news would mean something to me: every kidnapped child, every murder, every accident would haunt my thoughts severely. Regardless, I still feel it is necessary to know everybody. I would be invited to infinite amounts of birthday parties, weddings, and when abroad I would never feel out of place. How wonderful it would be to know every single soul.

My best friend would disagree. Right now she wishes she could disown all those she knows. Poor thing, in the middle of a divorce, who wouldn't want to be invisible in such a time? Well, maybe not invisible but rather in disguise. No one could survive the loneliness and neglect invisibility brings. But she should not be ashamed. A woman of such class should never give in. At least she keeps her dignity while she eats her tomato soup. She ensures that the spoon reaches her mouth, not the other way around. Ach, she will be just fine, I will let her vent as long as she wants. She can even cry in front of me I won't burst into tears. I am not one of those people who imitate for no reason. I never yawn when exposed to yawning. The only moment I imitate is when I am nervous. And God knows that never happens. Well, not never, I mean, it must have happened once before otherwise I would not have known that nervousness triggers my need to imitate. But since I can't recall the last time – or the first and only time it occurred, it is safe to say it never happens. It is only foolish for someone who has nothing to lose to feel nervous.

After lunch, if my best friend takes care of the bill, I will have spare coins to stop by the bakery and get some fresh bread for the pigeons by the lake. Just thinking about it makes me wish my best friend would drink and not eat her soup so that I can be on my way to save those precious pigeons from the hands of the civilized people. I cannot understand why they insist on feeding those creatures old bread. Even more puzzling is the pigeons eating the rotten thing! I nearly ate rotten bread myself once, but as soon as I noticed the green spot on the brown slice I quickly disposed of it in horror. Now, I know for a fact that those pigeons are not colorblind for scientists have been using pigeons in testing color perception long before I started watching all those documentaries. But of course if the pigeons were exposed to rotten bread since the beginning of time who am I to question their pickiness?

That is why I prefer the human race. Free choice. We can choose not to eat rotten bread. Still some claim, especially those old and tired philosophers, that we do not have free choice. That can't possibly be right. The only way we can draw such conclusions is if we knew our superiors and their free choice. We know our inferiors: we know the pigeons, and their limited choice. But do we know our superiors and their fresh bread?

My tuna sandwich is delicious. I love this restaurant. Clever are those who thought to put a restaurant in a department store. Women no longer need to visit two places to complete their shopping-lunch dates. Although I have noticed that many people only come here for the food. Now that is just odd. Why would one enter a department store to eat? If eating is your only mission you should visit a building solely designed to satisfy your hunger. Eating in this restaurant should be a privilege only enjoyed by those who truly intend to purchase an item from the store. No, better yet, *access* to this restaurant should only be granted to those who have proof of a purchased item, a receipt is most appropriate. There should be a security guard on the lookout for fashionable window shoppers who only walk about for five minutes heavily pretending to be searching for something, something precise and equally pretending not to have found it. After their disappointment they cheerfully head to the restaurant supposedly making their visit not entirely pointless. I spot three of them now, with their cups of tea and small pieces of cake – so transparent.

The restaurant trespassers are almost as transparent as my dear best friend. She has finished her soup and I can tell she feels much better than when we first entered the department store. Her soon to be ex-husband is still on her mind but she is capable of experiencing joy. And that is where most victims of divorce fail. They probably are not familiar with the shopping-lunch date remedy. I cannot think of one unwanted emotion that this activity cannot cure. You must have the shopping-lunch date with the right person though. I can feel the urge escape my body. I am convinced I can hold out another two weeks. Life has its ways of keeping you alive. As my dear best friend takes care of the bill I bow my head and giggle. We descend the escalator and head outside where it is raining. We share a warm embrace in front of the entrance of the department store. I turn left and head to the bakery, fishing the coins in my pocket. As long as I can experience joy I am fine.

A Keeper

Because I keep a mermaid in the basement
I wash her delicate sequined pink bra in the bathroom sink

gingerly scrub around her clam shells
with a soft toothbrush fresh out of its wrapper

Because I keep a mermaid in the basement
I have not done the work left me by a hurricane

She is a blue flame phosphorescence,
illuminating the basement in ways electricity never could

Because I keep a mermaid in the basement
I tell my nosy neighbors I am still waiting for FEMA
when they ask about the standing water and the flickering lights

Because I have named the mermaid in my basement, Jayne Mansfield
I have to rethink my sexuality

Jayne flips me her dorsal fin
swims deep and reads drowned books
learning the language they teach her

I tell her I will buy a wet suit
and take her back to the midnight ocean

Native Monsters

The first time Chris saw the centipedes crawling out from under his bed he was sure that it was all part of his imagination. Usually, during the night, he would close his eyes tight and try to make his bedroom turn into a jungle. But for the last few nights, whenever he closed his eyes to create the jungle out of the shadows cast by his nightlight, instead dangerous and horrible things would appear.

He hated centipedes the worst. Even though he knew they were imaginary, they still looked as awful as any centipedes he could remember seeing in movies or in books. They were everywhere now. But he wasn't going to be defeated by his imagination. Not tonight. He reached down and picked up one of the centipedes. His imagination told him that it was alive and crawling all over his hand. But he wouldn't be defeated. He took the centipede and put it in his mouth. He closed his mouth and dared his imagination to make him taste centipede.

~~~

She was his foster mother. This much he knew for sure. He had lived with her since the age of five. A very young age, indeed. It was hard to remember things before that age, but he did have vague memories of living someplace with other kids. If he tried hard enough, he thought he could recall a man, someone with a broad smile who was putting him up in a tree. There was nothing hostile about the action. It was the most natural thing in the world. This memory, however, was just a shadow in his mind, whereas the knowledge of his foster mother was real and ever-present.

At night she would stand in the door frame and just look at him. The soft glow cast by his nightlight made her into a silhouette. For a long time his imagination would work overtime. He would imagine her as some scary beast off in the distance. The room would grow into a jungle. He would slip past the beast, and then he would be off on a boat by himself. He was sailing off to an island. Yes, they would soon call him WILD THING. There he lived, free and unburdened by his old life. In his imagination, at this point, things became hazy. Magical, but still hopelessly obscure.

Then one night, the jungle didn't appear and his room filled with centipedes. The silhouette of his foster mother was still there—a terrible beast, but he was no longer able to go off into the jungle to find a boat. Instead, there was just the centipedes and her.

~~~

The taste in his mouth had been awful. Even if it was just his imagination turning against him there was nothing more real than the awful taste of centipedes. Now, as he was walking across the floor, he could feel the centipedes crawling between his toes and crunching beneath his feet. Still, he had to know whether he could reach the image of the silhouette in the background, whether he could put his hand against it and knock it down like some cheap cardboard cutout.

But when he was almost there, when the silhouette was big enough for him to reach out and touch, he found himself back in his bed. There was nothing there. Not even the silhouette. He was alone in a bed that existed in a vacuum, and all he could do was open his mouth. He tried to scream, but the vacuum swallowed up the sound of his misery and scattered it across a universe of nothing.

~~~

He wasn't sure what had happened, but his foster mother and father had stopped talking. In the morning the silence would drag on forever, and then finally, he would go to school. Something was happening, but at the age of 9-going-on-10 it was hard to know exactly what anything meant or if anything was real, or if he would just melt away. The mug his foster father drank from still said "Jesus Saves!" in big broad letters with an exclamation mark. He still put the same efficient energy into getting dressed every morning. His foster mother still got up early and made their breakfast every morning. But something had turned their

33

relationship, one of submissive loyalty by the wife toward the husband, strange and quiet.

It had been about a year since their real son, Tommy, had left to join the Army right out of high school. In a way Chris loved Tommy. It was Tommy who had sucked up the wrath of the two adults who had seemed constantly angry and constantly struggling to show their kids they were in control. Tommy's torture, he was sure, had been worse than his. At first, Tommy had bullied him. Such was the natural order of a child with an older brother. But as time went by, it was Tommy who had taught him how to survive. He showed him how to keep his mind busy with activities; how to avoid angering the two adults; how to avoid talking out of turn. More importantly, Tommy had given Chris the most important piece of advice through his actions: when it was time to go, it was time to go.

Outwardly, they tried to project themselves as kind and charitable. But as young as Chris was, he couldn't remember a time when he didn't think of his foster parents as angry people. Everything they did projected control. He avoided the new couch which was still wrapped in plastic to avoid stains. His cereal boxes would be thrown out and the cereal put in plastic containers to keep out germs. The house was clean beyond reason. There wasn't a day he didn't come home and his nostrils didn't burn from pine-sol.

These things he could handle on most days.

But lately, he would come home from school and the silence would fill up the house. He didn't know what to make of this silence, the anger that followed, any of it. He found himself going outside more and more to play. But he wasn't supposed to go anywhere beyond their block of the street. He found his stepmother watching him from the window. Some of the kids who were a year or two older than Chris would tell him that they were going down to the pier and asked if he would like to join them.

Chris couldn't. Not with his mother looking out the window at him.

34

Chris wasn't allowed to climb trees either. There was a large one in the front yard of the house with a long branch that extended outward. Once, in his boldness, he had asked if a swing could be put on it like their neighbors had a few yards down. His foster mother had looked at his foster father who replied simply, "No." When he asked if he could climb the tree, his foster father similarly replied with the same simple word. Instead, he looked at the tree and wondered if the vague memory of a man with a broad smile was a real memory or something he had made up.

~~~

They had always known that Chris was deviant. He had come that way from the orphanage. Sometimes his foster father would spank him over his misdeeds. Sometimes it was worse. But there was only so far they could go. Later he would realize that they were afraid of his case worker at the Department of Family Services. Sometimes Chris would have to read scripture out loud for hours. He couldn't pronounce all the words exactly right. But his foster father would stand and watch him, and then eventually, once he started crying, the man would say simply, "That's enough."

Chris had continued to suck his thumb throughout elementary school. Eventually though, after his foster father had weaned him off this practice through spankings and scripture readings, he would develop the habit of opening his mouth as wide as he could. He wouldn't scream for real. He would just pretend like the sound coming out of his mouth was an awful scream. First it was a scream of agony. Later, as he grew older, his scream would become a roar of defiance. He would open his mouth wide and try to let it out. Eventually, the jungle would appear in his dreams. He would go there, and with the monsters, with their horrible teeth and horrible claws, there was nothing but screaming and yelling.

~~~

Though he couldn't be sure, Chris thought that his foster mother had it worse. Sometimes he thought he could hear her whimpering in her room.

35

Sometimes he heard them arguing. His foster father wanted her to think only of the Holy Ghost, but the truth was that she would sometimes sit on the couch or on the porch and see ghosts. Not the holy kind, just ghosts.

And then one night, long before the silence started, he started to see the image of his foster mother as a silhouette at night in his door frame. At first he could imagine her as some kind of monster out in the distance. After a while, though, he couldn't imagine anything. She was just in the doorframe. Sometimes the centipedes would come and sometimes they wouldn't. Either way, he would open his mouth to scream—he would scream silently because he didn't have anything to counter the silence.

~~~

Then one day the jungle came to him without even trying. He had all but given up on his imagination. He half-expected his foster mother to come and stand in the door frame of his room, the nightlight casting an ominous glow. But she didn't. Instead, the jungle appeared, green and lush. He was a WILD THING again.

Suddenly, all of the other things seemed arbitrary, pointless. His mother coming to watch him at night. The angry silence of the house. The rules against him going past their street block. What did it all matter? He was a WILD THING. He found himself wading through the jungle. In the back of his mind, he knew he was really leaving the house. But what did he care? He knew he had been something before he came to this place. And now he would be that thing again. The boat would be waiting for him at the pier. It would take him to the island where he could continue his real life with the other monsters.

~~~

He had a backpack full of clothes. He took a few canned goods with pop top lids from the pantry along with some pop-tarts and some other snack food. He did this very quietly, but it occurred to him that if his foster mother or foster father found him, if they raised their voice, he would have no choice but to attack. He would fight to the death. There would be no other way.

It would all be over soon, he kept thinking. And then he was at the dock. But where he expected to find the boat, he instead found the monsters. Native monsters. With horrible teeth and horrible noses and horrible claws. The horrible monsters let out their horrible roars and gnashed their terrible teeth, but when it was all over he was still there. He roared the loudest, and they all cringed before him. It was just like in the book, only these monsters were real.

There were no menacing silhouettes that night. Under the dock, he slept in the cool air and listened to the ocean. He knew he couldn't hide forever. In the morning his foster parents would call the police and have them looking for him. Yes, his foster parents would find him. And they would scream and roar, but he would show them what they had feared all along. He would show them with his terrible roar and his terrible teeth, and more importantly, his terrible friends that he was the WILD THING. He would roar and go wild in ways that would make their silence impossible.

He would say things, and do things, and throw things that would make it impossible for them ever to take him back. And that was the point. They would take him to be with all the other WILD THINGS in the jungle where he belonged.

Tercet

Perhaps, because we knew that moments made
can be unmade and ruined utterly,
you and I embraced, and feared the silence –

lest it tempt us add one line too many

Growth

Roger first noticed the spot in the spring when he was thirty-four. It was not much bigger than a pencil eraser. It had the strangest color; like flesh, but not his flesh. It had a complexion all its own.

He prodded it, standing before the mirror every morning. It didn't hurt. In fact, he didn't feel anything at all. That was what worried him. It started as a smooth little nub, but as it grew, it began to look like a tiny ear, with intricate folds in the center, a little lobe at the bottom. He made a doctor's appointment.

"That's the strangest mole I've ever seen," his doctor said. "Still, I don't think you should worry. It doesn't look malignant. Just to be sure, I'll run some tests."

His doctor took out a pair of tweezers and a scalpel. Rubbed Roger with alcohol. "This may hurt a bit."

It didn't hurt. He took a shaving, fitted it snugly into a stoppered tube, and sent it off to the lab. Four weeks later, Roger got a voicemail. He should call his doctor's office at his earliest convenience.

"The test shows that your mole is completely benign," his doctor said. "You can of course have it removed, but there's no medical need to do so. Stop by my office if it changes shape or color, increases in sensitivity, or becomes otherwise bothersome."

Over the next several months, the growth matured until it really did look like an ear, growing there on his left side, halfway between his armpit and his hip. So Roger began talking to it. He told it of his life, growing up a farm boy in a small town in southern Michigan. He'd found it very difficult to adjust when he went to college in Chicago, where nobody knew anybody. After college, he moved back to Michigan, but mid-Michigan, for although he missed his family, his friends, he found the idea of going home distasteful. He was an accountant now, working in the state's capitol for a firm that handled corporate books.

Roger found himself confiding in his mole. He told it about his ex-wife, Jeanne. They'd had some terrible fights before the end. Jeanne had said he wasn't supportive of her career, he was too demanding, he didn't satisfy her sexually. She said it just like that too, enunciating it, *seck-shoe-lee*. When they'd met in college, she had been sweet and energetic. After graduation, she threw all her energy into her career. But she didn't have to be a career woman to impress him. All he'd ever wanted was someone to talk to, someone motherly. For the children. She did want children, didn't she?

He could remember it clearly, the day he'd finally asked her. They'd been married five months. He was sitting in his recliner, a book in his lap, and she was dusting the bookshelf nearby. She'd developed a habit of slouching and sighing when she was cleaning, like a child forced to stay indoors and do chores on a sunny afternoon. It was fall, and the trees outside were red and gold. The windows were open, probably for the last time this year, Roger thought. He could already feel a hint of northern chill in the air. Down the street, he heard kids laughing and screaming.

Someone should shut those kids up, Jeanne had said. Roger had said, they're just playing. It sounds nice. She said, it sounds like they're killing each other. Roger smiled at his book. He said she'd feel different when they're her own kids. And Jeanne had stopped dusting. She stared at him, one hand on her hip, the other holding the feather duster, limply. Roger asked, she *did* want kids? Jeanne scoffed: Why on earth would she? She had enough on her plate just cleaning up after him.

Telling this to the ear as he lay in bed, Roger had the strangest sensation. Like the ear had awakened at his side and was listening to him. It made him want to go on.

He'd tried to convince Jeanne to reconsider. They would make such beautiful babies: he with his blonde brawn, she with her fine features and slim shoulders. Boy or girl, they couldn't go wrong. They

40

could move to the country, where the kids would have room to grow. Wouldn't that be nice?

No, she'd said simply.

They didn't have to have children right away. Lord knows, there'd be time enough for that later on. But wouldn't she just consider?

No.

What about her parents? Surely they wanted grandchildren. Jeanne was an only child, her family's sole legacy. Wouldn't she like to see her family tree thrive? Wouldn't she like to have a little baby, and see it grow up right?

No. No. *No.*

Soon after, Jeanne insisted Roger use condoms, in addition to the birth control she was already taking. Roger refused. Condoms were for college kids. So Jeanne wouldn't sleep with him anymore. His own wife, and she wouldn't even sleep with him.

Telling all this to the ear comforted Roger. And why shouldn't it? It was like meditation, like talking to yourself in the shower, recalling all the details of your past. He grew attached to the ear, so that when it did change—it grew larger, paler—he hesitated to inform his doctor. He skipped his next physical for fear that his doctor would advise him to have it removed.

It occurred to Roger that he loved the ear. It was tiny and perfectly proportioned, a woman's ear, like a porcelain pink conch, so smooth, so delicate. He imagined what it would look like with an earring, a tiny gemstone like his mother always wore. His mother had never been a fancy woman; she didn't wear polish on her nails, she only wore dresses on Sundays or when company visited. But she almost always wore earrings. He thought perhaps he would like to buy earrings for the ear.

Weeks passed, and as the ear grew, Roger lost weight. Even so, he bought himself larger sport jackets, so that nobody could see the ever-growing lump protruding beneath the fabric. It was fully formed by that time, a third ear, sprouting out of Roger's side. Roger considered

41

it a blessing, remembering how lonely he'd felt since his divorce, how many times he'd thought *if only I had someone to talk to.*

And how resourceful, the human body! When Roger had needed, more than anything, a kind ear, his body had produced one for him! Roger lay in bed one night, rubbing lotion on the ear, for it had seemed a little dry lately. The ear was progressing steadily now, pulling away from his body until an extra bud of flesh had formed beneath it, raising it fully from Roger's side. A tuft of blonde hair sprouted at the edges. Roger lay stroking the hair.

"I think what I miss most is the simplicity of my old life," he said. "Living in the country, milking the goats in the morning, baling hay. The smell of freshly tilled soil in the spring, warm brown grass in summer. That was the worst part of Chicago—it was all concrete and traffic lights." He rolled onto his side, away from the ear. It stood erect against his torso.

"When I was a sophomore," he said, "I had a flower pot in my dorm room, and I planted grass seed in it. Not *grass* grass, just good old lawn grass. I watered it, trimmed it with scissors when it got long. I used to run my fingers through it," he told the ear, still stroking its hair.

A few weeks later, Roger got a promotion. During his performance review, Roger's boss praised Roger's improved performance over the past few months.

"Frankly, I'd had my doubts about you, Roger. But you've really pulled through for the company." Roger's boss clasped him on the shoulder. "Thanks to your efforts, we've taken on two big-ticket clients." As he dropped his arm, his hand brushed against the swell on Roger's side. It was as if his boss had never noticed before, even though by that time the growth protruded so much Roger's baggiest jacket pulled taught over the ear.

"Roger," his boss said. "What is that? Are you okay?"

"Nothing," Roger gave a dismissive wave. "Just a goiter or something."

"Oh," his boss said. "Well, then. Carry on."

~~~

Roger liked his new job, the added responsibilities. He liked adopting the farm-boy-makes-good persona. He came up with financial strategies for the new accounts, Jefferson Builders and R.H. Henley & Sons. At times, Roger was amazed at his own ideas. It was like they were being whispered to him from some higher power. He supposed it was just part of this therapeutic monologue he had with the ear.

The growth was now raised from his body on a lump like a pale grapefruit, having visibly doubled in size during the past month. A soft fuzz of wheat-colored hair covered the top of the dome, with indentations and a protrusion where eyes and a mouth might be.

And maybe Roger should have been disgusted by this thing that his body was budding. But he wasn't. He was elated. It was as if all his hopes and secret desires had leaked out through the pores on his side and were crystallizing there, like sap bleeding from an improperly tapped tree. The growth was sweet and pure and curative. He no longer felt alone; he had this perfect little bud on his side, everywhere he went.

He lay in bed one night and traced his fingers over the bump that could be lips. It moved. Independent of Roger's body, it twitched at his side. Roger sat up in bed. Slowly, rhythmically, he rubbed the peach fuzz on top of the growth. At first, nothing happened, but then Roger noticed cracks forming along the swollen lumps on the growth's surface. It trembled. It writhed. The cracks split open. Two eyes blinked up at him. The lips parted and breathed.

It never even occurred to him to see his doctor now, to have the growth examined. Intrinsically, Roger knew he had birthed something spectacular. She was striking, with full lips and brown eyes that stared up at him, considered him. She smiled, but the smile was broken by a pained expression, and she writhed again. Intentionally—at least it looked intentional to Roger—she pulled away from him. Roger felt nothing, but the expression on her face told him that the motion was excruciating. Her head angled away, and beneath it sprouted her own neck, fair and slender.

43

"Hello," he said, not knowing why he was whispering.

"Hello." She shook her head, and it expanded to the size of a child's head.

"Um, I'm Roger."

"Well, I know that," she shook her head some more. "I'm Helen." By now, her head was fully grown. She sighed, satisfied at having completed the task.

He stared at her. He grinned a crooked grin. "And are you—are you real?"

She cocked her head to one side. "What do you mean? I'm here, aren't I?"

"Yeah, I guess you are. But where did you come from?" His voice was still scarcely more than a whisper.

"Your side? Weren't you paying attention? I was in there, and then I pulled out, and now I'm out here."

"Right." And because he was at a loss for anything else to say, Roger craned his neck over to kiss her.

~~~

Roger took time off work. He had so much to do. First order of business, he had a tailor make a new wardrobe to accommodate Helen. He tried at first to cut neck holes in the sides of his tee shirts, but she wasn't satisfied.

"Roger, Honey, I have so little opportunity to express myself. It would be nice to be able to wear something a little pretty."

That made sense. So he bought starched men's shirts with the left sides stitched with frilly necklines or satin collars. It was a custom job, and the tailor charged him a fortune, but it was worth it. Now that Helen had bloomed, he abandoned his sport jackets. He didn't want to suffocate her. And anyway, she was too pretty to hide.

Within a couple days of her coming out, Helen's hair had grown and darkened to a deep chestnut brown. Roger bought two kinds of shampoo, since her hair was much finer than his. He switched soaps because his soap irritated her skin. He applied moisturizers morning and night. He wanted her to keep her youthful glow.

44

They decorated his house. Roger hadn't given his living space much thought, but Helen convinced him to feng shui the rooms. She instructed him on what to buy, rugs and candles and curtains. He quickly blew through his savings account, but he now had decorations hanging on his walls, a table cloth in the dining room, accent pillows on his couch.

Helen was a huge hit when Roger returned to the office. His coworkers all ogled her splendid features, her glossy hair and large, hopeful eyes. Roger was glad he had invested in the extra-body shampoo.

"So this is what you've been cooking up beneath those loose coats," his boss said to him. "Roger, you devil."

"What's your lady friend's name?" Hank from HR said.

Roger introduced her around. He watched as the men in his office, normally so reserved, became animated, giddy even. His boss talked louder, laughed more. Hank was more interested in chatting with Roger over lunch. Some of the other guys even stopped by Roger's office throughout the day, just to talk. Roger wasn't sure whether this was a good thing.

~~~

When Helen's cheeks started filling out, Roger learned to cook healthier foods—less steak and potatoes, more leafy green vegetables, things like that.

"This would be easier if you had some arms," he said one day while preparing a salad.

Helen nodded. She squeezed her eyes shut and flexed her facial muscles, widening her neck at the base. Her shoulders emerged. He watched as nubs budded on either side of her shoulders; they stretched into short, plump arms, ending in stumps. She had no hands. Roger couldn't help but stare now. He stared at her handless stumps. He'd asked for arms, and she'd grown arms. They didn't look like an amputee's, with the discoloration at the end, the bit of flesh tucked over and stitched. The ends were smooth, the skin undisturbed. It was unnerving.

45

"How about some hands?" Roger said.

"Oh. Sure." And she pushed hands out of her stumps. She hesitated for a moment, seemingly discontented. Then she shrugged her shoulders, scrinched up her face, and pulled, observing his figure and making the appropriate adjustments. He tried to remember when she had seen another woman, how she knew to make feminine curves. He didn't have a lot of women in his life; his office was kind of a boy's club. Yet somehow, Helen knew to form breasts, broad hips, round legs. He thought he saw a look of defiance in her eyes as she pulled out, detaching from him. And at the moment of separation, when she wrenched her body fully from his, he felt an emptying, a kind of loss deep inside him. He watched, helpless, as she fleshed out feet. She grew toenails.

"Maybe you should keep going," he said, noting that her legs weren't long enough to balance their thickness.

"No, this seems good," Helen said, and set about fixing dinner in the nude.

~~~

It didn't take long before Helen grew bored at home. She spent her time baking during the day, sent Roger to the office with cookies and quick breads, and when he got home in the evenings, she always had the table set with a sumptuous meal. This week alone she'd made them beef wellington one night, veal scaloppini the next, carne asada the night after that. Actually, she spent most of her time cooking, so that Roger missed being with her. He longed for the good old days when they would lie in bed, talking. He tried chatting with her while she was cooking, but she said he was hovering.

Roger had gained back all the weight he'd lost while Helen was still a bud on his side. Helen too seemed to be ripening to a voluptuous girth, her breasts straining beneath the fabric of her blouses, her stomach mushrooming over the top of her trousers. When she walked upstairs to the bedroom in the evenings, she was short of breath, and Roger couldn't help but envision her clutching her ample chest, falling backward, tumbling down the stairs a ways until he caught her, held her

46

in his arms, torn between holding her and running for the phone to dial an ambulance.

"What about chicken?" Roger said one night over dinner—steak au poivre with a red wine reduction, southern-style greens with bacon, and duchess potatoes. "You could make grilled chicken sometime."

"Sure , Honey. If that's what you like."

"And maybe a salad, or a stir fry. That might be nice." Growing up, he'd never lacked for fresh vegetables. His mother had sure known how to grow them.

He watched Helen spoon potatoes into her mouth. It bothered him that she used a spoon for such things, but then he supposed he should expect some eccentricities. She hadn't had the same upbringing he'd had.

"I've always wanted to make chicken salad," she said. "I saw a recipe in a magazine. It had walnuts and gorgonzola, dried cherries, an aioli dressing. You serve it on croissant, with a little lettuce leaf. How's that sound for dinner tomorrow?"

"Maybe you're missing the point," he said, slicing a bite of steak.

She laid down her spoon, and stared him down across the table. "What is the point?" She said quietly.

"It's just, I'm concerned for our health." Roger tried not to let his eyes dip down below Helen's neck.

"I'll schedule us each for a physical," she said with a placating smile.

He still hadn't been to the doctor, not since Helen was just a mole. He was terrified that if he went—moreover, if she went for a physical—the doctor would say something was wrong.

"What if you did that thing where you morph?" He waved his fork to indicate the general areas of her body. Hadn't he read somewhere that extra weight carried around one's waist was especially hard on the heart?

"It doesn't work like that." Her eyes pulled up at the corners as she spoke.

"How does it work then?"

47

"Didn't you ever take a physics class? It's conservation of matter."

"But you created matter."

She shook her head slowly. "I cook when I'm bored."

"So find something to do," he said. "What about gardening?"

Helen picked up her spoon. With potatoes poised and ready to enter her mouth, she announced, "I'm going to get a job."

It seemed like an empty threat to Roger. In this economy? What skills did she have? What could she possibly offer employers? But the next day, she went to the library, typed up her resume, asked Roger to proofread it while she cooked dinner. Under "Skills," she listed:

- *Increased office moral by introducing alternate, gender-specific personality traits to the workplace.*

- *Facilitated interpersonal relations in the office with the preparation of gastronomical offerings.*

- *Created financial plans for the Jefferson Builders and R.H. Henley & Sons accounts.*

"Wait just a minute," he said. "That was me. I did that."

"Really?" Helen said, swirling butter into a pan of beef glace de viande.

"Really," Roger said.

"All by yourself?" She said, ladling the sauce over thin-sliced roast beef.

Roger narrowed his eyes.

"Wasn't I there with you?" She said, scooping scalloped potatoes onto the plates.

She went to several interviews that next week, and in the evenings, Roger came home to messages on the answering machine. Places wanted to hire her immediately. To Roger's chagrin, she was hired as a line cook at some fancy pants restaurant downtown, where she started working nights, coming home long after Roger had gone to bed. In her absence, it seemed to Roger that his house was now too big. He sat in his chair in the evenings with all that space around him. He couldn't sleep without her. His bed was a fathomless expanse in which he twisted and stretched, feeling every ache in his body, every pore, as if it were magnified.

Something had to be done. Roger went to the jewelry store one evening, poured over the display case, his hands leaving sweaty prints on the glass. He settled on a solitaire, large and clear and indebting. Then he planned a trip home. He wanted his parents to meet the girl he'd hosted all those months. In early April, once the weather had broken, he packed up the car with gifts—a planter of Easter lilies for his mother, a tin of good pipe tobacco for his father, a little velvet box for Helen. This is what one does when a relationship stalls out: one plans for the next step.

As they drove away from the city, a sense of comfort eased over Roger. He watched the forest grow denser, the hills giving way to cornfields. He rolled down the window, breathed in the clean country air, smelling of grass and manure and spring breeze.

"Roger, Honey, can you put the window up? I'm freezing."

She huddled down in her seat, clutching her sweater higher around her neck. Roger had bought her a new outfit for the occasion, a pair of gray tweed pants and a turtleneck sweater, but Helen wore instead a pink cotton skirt, a sage green cardigan, a pair of sandals.

"It's so desolate out here," Helen said. "Nothing but corn and cows. Oh, I hope there's a decent grocery store in town. I don't know if I can make do with IGA."

How did she even know what IGA was? Maybe she'd heard it on TV, or read it in a magazine, some stuffy food publication poking fun at country bumpkins and their grocers. Helen had offered to cook dinner for his parents. It wasn't easy coaxing his mother into agreeing; normally, her kitchen was *her* kitchen. But Roger explained repeatedly that Helen was a wonderful cook, that it would help her feel at home.

"You know, Honey," Roger said. "My folks aren't really used to fancy cooking. You don't need to go out of your way for them."

"Kiss," she said. "K-I-S-S. Keep it simple, stupid." And she tittered to herself.

More and more, Roger noticed Helen's language deteriorating into catch-phrases and the gruff words used by men in kitchens. When Roger was in high school, he'd washed dishes at a local diner. The boys in the kitchen weren't exactly the most eloquent, and it pained him to hear her take on their speech patterns.

They stopped at a grocer on the way, because his home town did only have IGA. The one time he wanted her to cook beef and potatoes, and she bought lamb to roast with apricots and mint, balsamic vinegar to glaze carrots, and something called quinoa. Roger had never heard of it before, and he could be sure his parents wouldn't have either.

When they finally made it to his folks' house, his parents were waving from the porch, his mother in a long rust-colored dress, his father in old jeans and an older tee shirt. As Roger pulled up the driveway, there was a white goat lying in the middle of the path. Roger stopped the car and blew his horn. The goat stared him down through the windshield until Roger got out of the car to shoo it away. When he turned back to the car, he caught sight of Helen through the windshield. Her smile seemed forced. She was eyeing the couple on the porch, noting the small farm house, judging the barns with their paint chipped away, their weathered gray wood revealed. Even though the trees were beginning to bud, the grass hadn't quite greened up yet. Perhaps he should have held out until the trees were dark with leaves and the grass was full of wildflowers. Roger had lived here long enough to know the whole state looked a little tattered by winter's end. As he got back in the car, he considered what Helen must have thought of the dirt driveway, the scrawny goat standing now on the side of the road, ruminating. Seeing his parents' farm through Helen's eyes, he could relate to the expression on her face. The sun shone on the goat, accentuating its dingy fur, and it winked one eye in the glare, as if it were cluing them in on some secret.

"Mom, Dad," Roger said, standing on their front porch, balancing a bag of groceries on one hip. "I'd like you to meet Helen." With his free hand on the small of her back, he nudged her forward.

"Bout time you brought a woman home," Mom said, looking up into Helen's eyes. He'd never realized how short his mom was. Had she shrunken over the years? "Your father and I were beginning to wonder. Soft hands," she said as she shook with Helen. Roger suspected this was a criticism.

"I brought gifts," Roger offered, handing the groceries to his mom, then going to the car to retrieve the luggage. Once inside the house, Mom fussed over the lilies, placing them first on the small kitchen table, where they took up much of the space there, then on the counter, and finally settling on a spot on the coffee table in the family room. Dad thanked him for the tobacco, and tucked the tin away in a drawer. Roger saw other tins in the drawer as well, presents from past years, unused, forgotten.

~~~

Roger and his dad sat in the family room, drinking beer while his father smoked his usual pipe and read the paper. Roger listened anxiously as the women murmured in low voices in the kitchen. His mom offered to help cut up vegetables, asked why Helen did things this way or that, tended to the roasting meat when Helen's back was turned. She offered Helen another glass of lemonade cut with vinegar.

After a while, Roger's mom came into the family room. She looked suddenly old to Roger, grey and frail, and her hands were thin and veiny as she wiped them on her dress. Roger's dad shook his newspaper, folded it back up and tucked it under his chair. He leaned forward in his seat a moment, his hands resting on his knees, then stood, and left the room. Roger wondered, perhaps for the first time ever, whether this was how a normal family operated. His mom and dad seemed to him like similarly charged magnets, incapable of occupying the same space. It had been like this his whole life; he couldn't ever remember his parents sitting together, having a conversation, working on a common project.

"I'm getting in that poor girl's way," Mom sighed, and settled herself onto the couch. She picked up a basket from the floor, and pulled from it her latest needlework project. "I suppose it's nice to be

51

taken care of," she said. "Roast lamb," she added. "I've never had that before."

At dinner, Roger didn't know which was worse: the look on Mom's face as she picked at her food, or the fact that Dad cleaned his plate and then held it out for seconds.

~~~

Whenever there were four people together in his parents' house, there must be a game of euchre. This evening was no exception. Helen and Dad partnered together. Roger knew it was more than just a friendly game. It was a test to see how well Helen fit into the family. He'd been worried that she wouldn't pick up on the intricacies of the game. Dad had told Helen only the basic rules, without delving into strategy. Yet, in an inexplicable stroke of beginner's luck, Helen and Dad were walloping Roger and Mom.

Roger supposed he should be pleased. Helen seemed to be bonding well with at least one of his parents. But deep down, Roger felt cast aside in favor of a new toy. Roger often felt this way with his dad, as if he didn't measure up. He always assumed it was because his dad thought him effeminate, for while Roger had the brawn of a good farm boy, he also had a gentleness to him. He cried sometimes when watching movies or reading books. He enjoyed art and music. His feelings could be hurt. But as Roger watched Dad interact with Helen, all of his notions of what his dad preferred came into question. Helen was soft, round, fair, feminine, emotional, sometimes crying for no good reason at all.

The second game, Roger dealt the first hand. He picked up his cards, studied them. Jack, ace, queen, and ten of spades, and the jack of clubs. A loner hand. The card he'd turned up was a heart. He felt his stomach tighten. Then his dad, his mom, and Helen each passed, and Roger turned the card over. What were the odds it would come back around to him, that he would be able to call trump? As he assessed the table, he realized his dad was watching Helen. He saw Dad rub his wedding ring. And Helen glanced at her cards, then shook her head subtly.

"Pass," Dad said, nonchalant.

Unbelievable. That was blatant table-talk. They were only on their second game, and already Helen was comfortable enough with strategy to use it to her advantage. Roger also noticed that Helen moved her left arm languorously, gingerly. Did she have cards up her sleeve? She seemed reluctant to drop her arm, holding it away from her body as if she were sore or injured. Roger wanted to call them on it, wanted to alert his mom to their trickery. Then again, wasn't the point of this visit to get his parents' approval before he proposed to Helen? His mom didn't believe in cheating. But neither did his dad, Roger had thought.

Mom took her time, seeming to hesitate over her cards. How could he tell his mom to call spades, Roger wondered? Mom pulled a card from her hand, and tucked it back in in a different spot. *Spades*, he thought loudly. If only she would look up at him, he could mouth the word.

"Pass," Mom said at last, and Roger felt the air go out of him. He glanced over to see Dad nod.

"Hearts," Helen said. "Alone," she said, and Dad set his cards on the table, face down. Although Roger had missed the motion, he knew without a doubt that Helen had put her hand to her chest, perhaps traced the two lobes joined in a point, motioning to Dad before Dad had nodded. Roger's face felt hot.

Roger expected Helen to end it quickly, laying her cards down in one smooth motion. Instead, she dragged it out, playing her cards one round at a time, a little flourish of her wrist each time she laid the card that would take the trick.

"I like this one," Dad smirked as Helen raked in the cards with both hands. She then added four points to their score.

Roger fumed for the rest of the game, unable to concentrate he was so annoyed. After Helen and Dad won the second game, Roger feigned fatigue.

"I might just hit the hay," he said, yawning loudly, when Dad suggested another game.

"It's only nine o'clock," Dad said. "Don't be a pansy."

Roger insisted. It had been a long drive, a long week. He was ready to turn in.

Mom put Roger and Helen in separate rooms. After Mom made both beds with fresh sheets, Roger listened as she descended the stairs. He felt like he was in college again, before he and Jeanne were married, when they'd first visited his parents. They'd wait for hours until he was certain his parents had gone to sleep, and then he'd sneak into Jeanne's room, careful not to tread on the floorboards he knew to squeak. They'd lay a blanket out and make love on the floor, because the bed frame was also squeaky. Then they'd lie together until the rooster crowed at dawn, when Roger would sneak back into his own room.

Which was all good fun when he was twenty-something. But at thirty-something, it seemed absurd. His parents had to know he and Helen lived together. Did they think Helen had a separate room in Roger's house? It was ten thirty before all was quiet downstairs. Roger crept across the hall. Light leaked into the hallway from beneath Helen's door. He knocked quietly before entering.

Helen was seated as the brass vanity, rubbing moisturizer onto her face. "Roger, Honey. It's late. Do you need something?"

Roger closed the door behind him. He watched her for a while. He'd always wondered what took her so long to get ready for bed, but he'd never felt allowed to enter the bathroom when she was in there. She finished with the lotion, and fished a hair brush out of her makeup bag.

"What was that tonight?" Roger tried to keep his voice down.

"What was what?"

"You and my dad were cheating," Roger said. He had his back to the door.

A slow smile slid onto Helen's face. "Are you sore we won?"

"You were table talking, Helen. That's dishonest."

"I have no idea what you're talking about." Helen was slowly brushing her hair, moving with hesitation, as if her side were still hurting her.

"That's another thing," Roger said. "Did you have cards up your sleeve?"

"Don't be ridiculous," Helen said, still brushing her hair awkwardly.

"You did," he said. "You still do."

"Roger, you're paranoid."

He moved into the room now, standing beside her. He pulled her out of her seat by her arm. "Let's see them," he said, pushing her sleeve up to her elbow.

"Let go of me," she said, and jerked away from him, cradling her left side. "What the hell's your problem?"

"I want to know what you're hiding," Roger said.

Helen opened her mouth, sighed, and closed it again. She was still holding her side, and Roger envisioned an entire deck of cards hidden up her shirt. Had she and his dad conspired before the game started? How could they have coordinated it so they had the cards they needed? Roger's head was spinning. It was all too much.

Slowly, with the same kind of triumphant flourish Helen had used every time she took a trick at cards, she lifted her shirt. Roger waited for the cards to fall, but they didn't. Nothing fell. He leaned in for a better look. He gasped.

There, on Helen's left side, halfway between her armpit and hip, a tiny pink ear was growing. It didn't look anything like Roger's ear.

"Are you—pregnant?" He said.

Helen glared at him. "Does it look like I'm pregnant?" She said. "Surely you know how a pregnancy works."

Roger sat down on the bed. He leaned forward so far that his head was almost between his knees. "I don't understand," he said. But he did understand. Before he even finished the statement, reality hit him like a collision of astrological bodies. Helen was, this vary minute, conglobing new life on her side. It was more than a pregnancy, because it was in no way intentional. It was essential. He felt suddenly heavy, as if the gravity of the room had increased. It anchored him to the bed, and his eyes fell level with her growth, the pale pink ear, the freckled lobe, its curving dark hollow rimmed with soft fuzz. It was a spiral wending into the unknown, folding in on itself like a dark galaxy.

Cracked Buttons

Exiting my building, I good morning Harvey, my blue uniformed doorman. Instead of good morning back, his eyes scream and mouth sputters. I look myself over: Am I bleeding? Did I forget my pants? No. I turn toward the lobby mirror for the larger view. There's none of me there. Only General George S. Patton. Starched greens and starred helmet. Face clenched. Taller than expected.

Harvey's wavering salute never reaches his forehead, face switching back and forth between me and Patton, panicked as if all his holiday tips are in jeopardy, and saying, "I, I, I—" Patton scowls. "What's that jackass hand maneuver, soldier?" He unholsters a pearl handled pistol. "Whoa," I say. "We're men of peace." "You're men of lemon meringue," he says and shoots Harvey in the chest.

"Maniac!" I yell at Patton. "He's the best doorman we've ever had. When my shirts come back from the cleaners, he always calls my apartment. I don't even have to come down. He hooks them on the elevator railing. Doors open and they're waiting. Just like in my closet!" Patton holsters his pistol. "If I don't lead, they won't follow." He walks straight as a lamppost into the mirror's falling horizon.

I lean over Harvey. The corners of his mouth can't hold up his smile. Eyes running out of sight. He says, "I work with the public. I do what I can. I try to stay happy." I speak as if praise could hold onto a necessary life. As if pleading could. "You're great at your job. I miss you already. My cleaning misses you. My shirts. All those cracked buttons."

The Wrong Word

"Asshole."

Once it was out, I could see the anger, the outrage well up in his blackened eyes. It wasn't a word coming from me. It was a characterization, a condemnation—as if I insulted his heritage and degraded whatever courage it took for him to come to this country, this city, and the place where he stood in his pressed blue uniform, representing one of the most prestigious cultural institutions in the world.

"You can walk. I can see you walk." He repeated this several times in an accent, possibly Jamaican, until I could no longer control my temper and brand him an asshole.

There wasn't much else to it, and yet it was everything. Of course, he didn't know that at the time. He couldn't have. He was doing a job, maybe a new job that would pay for a place where his parents could come and live, or to support his growing young family.

The Metropolitan Museum on Fifth Avenue and 82nd Street, a 13-acre scrap of land nestled into the eastern side of 843 acres of Central Park had a roof garden where, weather permitting, you could go for cocktails on Friday evening or stroll next to an exhibition of international artists. This summer, Franks Stella's massive polished metal pieces filled the garden space. I usually came up here with Charlie Martin, a friend from work, on Friday nights. It was a way to end the week, socialize, and simply relax. It defined the beginning of the weekend.

Charlie's job was to get on one of the two torturously slow moving cocktail station lines and bring back drinks and chips; usually one bag, though more recently two. I was tasked with getting seats on one of the dozen wooden benches scattered around the sculpture garden.

Most of the time I was successful in spite of the hordes of tourists that were delighted to have found a sanctuary amid Manhattan's relentless concrete landscape. And there was an abundance of women—young and European and every once in a while, older and flirtatious.

If they sat down next to us we would be fast friends in minutes, especially Charlie whose passport looked like a roadmap of the world, having explored places so far off the beaten trail in Asia that it took special guides and a cocktail of immunological shots to get him in and out.

It was an hour and a half infused with observations about politics, the deterioration of modern culture, the rise of a virulent religious right, and how we had dealt, successfully or not, with the options life had set in our path.

By the time I wanted to get off the roof that Sunday afternoon, I had been sitting alone for over an hour, the guard near the elevators demanded everybody leave through a new exit at the far end of the roof garden. "You can't use the elevator to get down now. They are closed to go down."

At first, I didn't understand him, or the concept. I noticed one of the two elevators waiting open not ten yards away. Visitors were being turned back as I continued in the direction of the elevator bank and, as the guard's voice became more insistent.

"The elevators are for people coming up now. You must go that way," he said, motioning toward the small entranceway in the opposite direction.

"I can't use the stairs."

"You must use the stairs. Go that way," he said, pointing.

He didn't understand and, resenting the need to explain or defend, I responded, "I can't. I have bad knees."

"You can use the stairs. Everybody has to use the stairs."

"I can't walk down stairs."

"Yes, you can walk. I can see you can walk."

"You don't know that I can walk down stairs."

59

"You can walk. I can see you walk."

I stood in silence.

"I see you can."

I raised my voice. "You're not a doctor, you're an asshole. And I am using the elevator."

"Don't call me an asshole," he shot back, as a pair of Italian tourists quickly turned away.

It was exactly what I wanted to say, at least before I said it. I continued walking toward the empty elevator.

The guard ran past me demanding that the elevator operator not take me down, adding that he was going to call security. As he walked away, I told the attendant with her hand on the controls to take me down. "Hit the down button," I demanded. "Hit it now, young lady."

She stood frozen. We were the only two in the elevator.

"Take me down right now."

Her face darkened with anxiety. "I will get into trouble." The accent was distinctly Eastern European.

This was going to get out of control and ugly, and I wasn't interested in the guard telling his side of the story to security before I had a chance to tell mine.

I moved into the other elevator that was now occupied by a half dozen tourists who had walked into the empty elevator as the guard abandoned his post to call security. The guard turned, saw me, and walked back and got up to my face, and angrily announced, "I am not an asshole."

"Call security right now. Go. Right now," I demanded defensively, and walked into the elevator with the group of shocked spectators. The guard turned on the second elevator operator, demanding that he too not take me down.

In the present insistence of an elevator full of people, he shut the oversized steel doors in the guard's enraged face. I went directly to the security desk on the main floor.

60

"Who do I speak to regarding an incident I just had with a security guard on the roof?" I asked the middle-aged man and younger woman sitting behind the security desk near the entrance to the museum.

The woman behind the desk agreed the guard had gone too far. Mark introduced himself as the security manager. At well over six foot, rail-thin, calm, and confident, he looked like a very capable cop who had taken early retirement. He also thought it was an unfortunate incident and apologized.

I made it clear that I didn't want to register a formal complaint. Mark asked if I would tell the story to the head of security. He thought it would be helpful, and not out of the usual when, "things like this happened." I said I would. He wrote down my name and number. Sounding satisfied that my complaint was given the necessary respect; I thanked them and got as far as the steps outside the front of the museum leading down to Fifth Avenue.

My name and phone number was sitting on a stranger's desk, and when the head of security called I would have to include the fact that I had called one of his own an asshole, ostensibly, for doing his job. There are usually several sides to any story, and the one that invariably wins out is the one that's told first, and with the greatest passion.

The front of the Metropolitan Museum of Art that sits astride Fifth Avenue is one of the wealthiest and most prestigious neighborhoods in the city and probably the country. An elegant throwback to the days of the robber barons, one of whom was J. P. Morgan, who helped to create the institution in 1870, along with businessmen and financiers as well as leading artists and thinkers of the day—visionaries who wanted a city museum of stature and grandeur that would bring art and art education to the American people.

In an age of identity theft, on-line access to the minutest personal detail of a person's background, I was convinced that what I had done was stupid and dangerous. This information was more likely than not going to find its way to friends of the guard on the roof.

I envisioned reprisals. Phone calls in the night, people appearing on my block that obviously didn't belong there. Threats from the ether.

61

I followed a handful of Dutch tourists through the doors and walked back over to Mark. "I think I would rather not have anyone follow up on this. I'd like to get that piece of paper back."

"I already called the head of security," he said, holding out the scrap of paper as if it was now part of a greater internal archival database that in time would reveal the truth—asshole and all.

"Then I'll wait to hear from the Chief of Security," I said, unable to take my eyes off the scrap of paper which contained enough information for someone to find, stalk, and strike out at me.

"We do this all the time, sir."

"Yes. Then thanks again. Mark? Right?"

"Mark Hammond."

Outside, vendors hawked sodas, ice crème, t-shirts, hats and hot dogs, hand-painted silk scarves, framed and unframed prints and paintings, brushed metal animal figurines, and Matryoshka nesting dolls and more recently, copies of the most popular movie screenplays.

The steps were crowded with tourists making my normal diagonal, zigzag decent impossible. And I had no intention of returning to the elevators to take me down to the street level. I grasped the polished brass handrail and descended, one foot slowly following the other, thinking that if the guard from the roof saw me barely maneuver, awkwardly, painfully, step-by-step, he might understand what it was like to have knees that had long ago lost their lifetime warranty.

I saw the guard's face many times in the following days. He cursed me to his family and his friends. He had been insulted. He couldn't walk away from the incident. His culture wouldn't let him. The eyes of his family and friends would accept nothing short of regaining his respect.

I sensed him waiting for the right time to call from a street phone in a nondescript neighborhood.

I iced down my knees that night, as I had most every day of every month for decades. In the week that followed, I worked from home, staring at the fire escape on the other side of my window.

"Guys like that don't rat out their own." Charlie said, "They'd probably rather not report incident, especially when there was no formal complaint."

To them, I was another indignant tourist going back to Omaha or Oslo in a few days; even if the phone number I gave them was local.

Charlie came by my office the following Friday during lunch and asked if I wanted to go to the museum after work. I gave him a confident thumbs-up without taking my eyes off a draft of a strategic plan I was preparing for an electronics company.

The clarity of my report slipped away, replaced with the image of a man curled to his knees, waiting on my roof. From there my apartment was one flight down the fire escape.

The man wore an old, heavy tool belt around his waist. A hammer and tape measure hung from the worn leather loops positioned above his right hip. The torn grey coveralls and paint scarred white t-shirt were authentic. He was in his late twenties, about 5'8", 170 pounds. He was clean-shaven with short hair. There were no visible scars or pronounced features. The beginning of a tattoo drifted from under his right shirtsleeve. From the look of his hands, you would have thought physical labor was something strange to him.

I felt my face flush. My fingers began to tingle. I reached for the phone, dialed Charlie's extension. Anxiety attacks happen without warning and that quickly. He came in and shut the door. I reached for a bottle of water on my desk. My head fell back against the chair and the bottle slipped from my grasp.

"This is fuckin' crazy, man. It's all about nothing." Charlie picked up the half-empty plastic bottle of water.

"I saw him on my fire escape."

"When?" he asked, taken aback with the authority of my claim.

"Just now."

"You can see from Wall Street up to the museum, with all the traffic and through the fuckin' hundred-story buildings? You can see through it all to the back of that mansion of yours to your fifth-story

63

fire escape? And what was he wearing, a ski mask, a black cape, or was he a real pro with a Spiderman or Batman costume?"

My panic attacks came a few times a year and lasted between 30 and 60 seconds, leaving me uneasy, and often totally exhausted. I've heard of people having attacks that lasted minutes, ones that left them incapacitated for hours.

I pressed for a deep breath. "I know. It's stupid."

"Killing yourself is not stupid. You know, sometimes I've even encouraged it. Scaring the shit out of me, that's stupid."

After a week of roiling anxiety, I had to believe the guard was not lurking on my fire escape, or had already made his way past the shattered window pane next to my desk and into my closets, drawers, smashing valuable artifacts and personal belongs, pissing on my bed, and pocketing my checkbook and laptop, or simply waiting to greet me when I got home.

I picked up my mail and stepped into the elevator and hit the fifth floor button feeling many years older than fifty-three. I got to my front door, keys in hand, and paused to listen for noise coming from within. I unlocked the door and pushed it open. The laptop was where I had left it. The windows were intact and my dresser drawers were closed. I fell back on my bed. I had a half an hour before I was meeting Charlie.

"Asshole," I murmured a few times. I didn't like the way it sounded.

It was a few minutes after 5 p.m. when I reached the museum. At the far end, a painted juggler worked coins from the crowd. Children giggled with curious delight. I was determined to make the most of the evening. Charlie bounded up the steps. A dozen years ago, he'd had a triple bypass. After the surgery, he became a vegetarian model of moderate exercise walking for an hour at a brisk pace at 5 o'clock every morning.

I took my time slowly working diagonally up the steps. We went in and flashed our membership cards at the information desk. They had seen us here many times. We looked the same age, were pretty much the same weight, and had gracefully graying hair. Charlie was a few inches taller.

"Jean isn't here," he said.

"Probably too early for her shift," I said turning towards the security desk. I walked back over to Mark Hammond who was responding to a tourist's question. He spotted me and smiled. "How are you?"

"I'm fine, but your head of security never called."

"I'm sorry. I know he got the message."

Hammond had an easy, Southern way about him. A guy that never got flustered or emotional. I could use tutoring in both, though I was probably projecting more on him than he deserved. "I'm disappointed."

"Do you want me to call him now?" His offer was genuine.

"No," I answered. The issue and the opportunity to deal with it had past. "Thanks for your help."

I made my way back to the information desk where Charlie had found the youngest and blondest intern to flirt with. It was easy for us. He preferred tall thin blondes who were embarrassingly young, while I pursued dark, Mediterranean types with deep, arresting curves.

The walk to the elevators that would take us up to the roof garden wound through the galleries of Medieval Art, European Sculpture, and Decorative Arts. There was short line in front of the elevators. We waited less than a minute and were pitched up to the fourth floor in seconds.

Charlie raced on line to get drinks and I walked over to a couple seated on each side of a sleeping young boy. By the time he had gotten drinks, they had picked up the sleeping child and offered me their space. I nodded appreciatively and sat down.

"Here, relax." Charlie handed me my wine and a bag of barbecued chips. "He's not here."

"How do you know?"

"You would have spotted him right off and said something to me."

I lifted my plastic cup, "To Fridays."

65

"To Fridays and women in slight summer dresses."

The wine was adequate, the chips really delicious. An hour passed. The place started to fill up and by six; there were long lines at both cocktail stations. The roof garden was packed with couples, women in groups of two and three, and tourist's agape at the charm and vitality of the space and power of the artwork.

Frank Stella's recent installation on the roof was drawing awe and praise. Many didn't quite know what to make of his art. However, it was Stella and that name commanded time and, in the end, considered respect.

Had I spent the week in wasteful anger and anxiety? I reacted as I did for a generation of reasons, some obvious, many rooted in places I generally didn't expose to the yellow of day, not the least of which was a stranger telling me about myself that was a painful impossibility. Maybe I should have spent the week chronicling with justification how great I once was as an athlete or how agile I had been in bed before my surgeries?

After so many years I had become a stranger in the mirror.

I hadn't been made a cripple or had my innards surgically reconfigured, but I wasn't all I had been either. And I was the only one who understood that. And that was twenty-three years ago.

A young woman sat down next to Charlie and he quickly struck up a conversation. She was at least thirty, thin, with a light German accent, and no noticeable curves.

I started my deep breathing exercises, determined not to let the stress build up, determined not to have a second panic attack. Between the wine and the deep breathing, I spotted a shapely brunette, regrettably in a conversation with an all too slick European type on the other side of the large red Stella.

I walked the perimeter of the garden that I guessed was about 10,000 square feet of open space, bounded on the eastern side by a wall trestle of ivy and open to the vistas of Central Park below on the other three. The attendants at the two refreshment stations were working feverishly to understand the dozens of languages and translate them into drinks, smiles, and cash.

By the time I returned, the German had abandoned Charlie whose smile told me he had come away with more than her name. Then I noticed the brunette was drinking alone, and in the same sweep, two men in uniform wheeling a wagon loaded with bottles of wine, ice, boxes of chips, utensils, napkins, and towers of plastic cups approach the refreshment station near the elevators.

He was one of the two guards walking directly behind them.

"What, were, the, fucking odds?" I dialed Charlie. "There are two guards at the refreshment station near the elevator. It's the young black guy."

Charlie got up instantly. "Right. Doesn't look like much, does he?"

"One day the face of a choir boy, the next, he offs his grandparents with a butcher knife."

Charlie walked toward the refreshment station. I dialed his number again. He made no attempt to respond. The brunette made her way past Charlie and the refreshment station and disappeared into the crowd.

Charlie walked up to the front of the line and made a pretense of getting napkins for his drink. He spoke to a couple at the head of the line and in seconds, they were nodding and laughing. He pocketed the napkins, turned past the two guards, and walked back to the bench.

I made my way to the far end of the roof and leaned over the railing overlooking the park. My phone rang. "Why don't we get something to eat?"

"Great idea."

"I'll meet you downstairs at the information booth."

"What do you mean?"

"I mean I'm not walking past him with you."

"See you downstairs."

Charlie slipped his phone into his pocket and walked toward the elevator. I walked in the opposite direction, towards the narrow set of stairs that I swore I couldn't manage. The corridor was claustrophobic and thankfully, not crowded. I went down the flight to the third floor feeling every painful, cautious step.

By the time we got to the Vietnamese restaurant, Charlie was insisting, "The guy probably forgot what you said."

Four times he demanded—no, insisted, "I am not an asshole." How many times since then had he repeated the insult? Would he ever forget?

Halfway through dinner I felt the tips of my fingers start to tingle, my face quickly flush. This time I fought back. I simply would not let the anxiety, the demons that existed deep within, take hold. I had been feeding the monster for years in a hundred different ways with incidents far less noteworthy, though few seemingly more regrettable. I believed the beast was going to come to the surface one day and not be satisfied with merely scoring a thirty-second panic attack.

After dinner, Charlie walked toward his building and I walked three blocks further south along Third Avenue, towards mine. I had work to do this weekend, and my dentist's niece was in town. He was eager for me to meet her. I was taking Carol to dinner tomorrow and looking forward to the distraction.

A young couple came out of a local comic club, laughing and holding each other. I watched them walk into the street, hail a cab that disappeared into traffic. As I rounded the corner of my block, I noticed a late model sedan pulled up at a fire hydrant in front of the building next to mine. It was old. There was rust along the bottom of the front door. The paint was worn and badly scratched. Two men were seated in the front.

The driver was smoking. They were wearing undershirts. A man in the back seat sat motionless. From where I was standing at the corner of my block, they could have been any age. The front door on the driver's side was a few inches ajar. I crossed to the south side of the street behind the car and walked toward my building.

It was well past 10 o'clock.

The long green canopy jutting out from the face of my building to the street gave the impression that there were people of substance inside. It was true, but that was a century ago, when the building was constructed. Now, there were mostly working couples and upwardly mobile singles happy to have eat-in kitchens and a little extra closet space in a city absent both. I had lived here and been married and divorced here and had once been very much younger here, and had my first panic attack here.

As I crossed the street I heard an engine cough to life. The driver shifted gears, the car moved slowly away from the fire hydrant. There was a fourth man in the car.

The superintendent of my building opened the front door for Ms. Robbins, a nice woman who had celebrated her 88th birthday a week ago. He nodded towards me, forgetting that he was supposed to have called last week to repair my bathtub faucet.

What I heard next was the crack of a pistol shot directly behind me. What I felt was a searing pain across my back that exploded through to my chest. I looked down, eyes wide with panic and grasped my shirt, expecting to see a gaping wound gushing blood. Instead I saw the superintendent race to catch me as I pitched forward, right before the side of my head struck the edge of the front door and I lost consciousness.

Voices faded and returned. The paramedic, my super, maybe neighbors. The wailing ambulance ride to the hospital only a dozen blocks away. A doctor in the hospital cracked orders to expand my IV line. Muffled voices about how the backfire of an old muffler in a car driven by construction workers after they picked up a friend from a jobsite, exploded in the street had sent my heart into cardiac arrest.

"Find out if he has any relatives," a young woman's voice demanded.

There was no wound. I hadn't been shot. They were waiting to stabilize me before they proceeded with additional tests. I heard this through bubbles and haze. The pain in my chest was merely noteworthy, compared to the constant piercing in my neck. The thick bandage over the laceration and five stitches on the right side of my forehead attested to the impact of my fall against the sharp edge of the metal door.

Charlie stopped off later that evening after calling me a half dozen times to see if I survived the walk home and found out what had happened. Besides the neck brace to keep me from doing further damage to my fifth and sixth vertebrae, I was not in good shape. My blood chemistry was so out of whack, the doctors wondered if I had suffered a silent heart attack earlier in the day.

I hadn't been shot, though my body was reacting as though I had been severely traumatized. The real me had been revealed. The real me, riddled with debilitating fears and doubt, had rendered me fragile and vulnerable far beyond my years.

I remembered I had to water my plants, get paper for my printer, and fresh fruit for breakfast. I had to pick up my dry cleaning in the morning, buy a lottery ticket. and check out what the 11 a.m. gallery talk was about at the Met, and this time, try to get in a few minutes of relaxing meditation before I went to bed.

I remember a nurse coming into my room later that night and telling me they were going to hold off on tests until tomorrow, and asked if my brace was comfortable. My vital signs and blood chemistry were slowly improving.

The neck brace limited me to a great view of shadows on the ceiling, and little else. The pain meds made a slow motion mush of most of the words that floated by me, and the concerned faces that eased up to the side of my bed.

I also remember, I guessed it was even later that night, the spray of light from the doorway of my hospital room expand across the ceiling, then quickly shrink back to nothing.

Electronic monitors blinked away at my side, protecting me from my own madness. I forced up a first, deep, relaxing breath, then another when a voice whispered in my ear in an accent I couldn't quite place, "asshole," just before something very hard slammed down on my chest. Once. Twice.

The faint shadows on the ceiling now moved violently, arms gesturing, threatening.

Four times. I soon lost count.

I spent the last few moments of my life trying to figure out what had happened, with fleeting regrets that I was going to disappoint my dentist and stand-up Carol, right before darkness rushed in and overwhelmed me.

Fear

It never goes away, it only diminishes,
thins out like a bookmark you forget
in one of the books you now rarely read.
Then you find it while dusting one day.

It springs out voluptuous, huge—this
bosomy aunt who always arrives
out of nowhere to stay, suitcases and all,
who manifests her love
by crushing your face against
the solid breasts, the loudly thumping heart.
When she's done, you're done with.

She takes you by surprise, yes.
She doesn't kill you,
though death might seem preferable.
You start eating your meals together.
She sips from your tea, shares
your bed at night, comfortably curled in
between you and your husband, in the crook
of his arm, in the warm dip of your thigh—
incestuous, fascinating.

Like an old dog, she slathers you with her drool,
and you'll never understand why
your husband takes you so lightly
when you say you hate that.
He laughs it off and you seethe.
You feel murderous. You

go off to some room to drown
your unhappiness in folding laundry,
or else, yelling at your children.

The fear is there, folding along with you,
carefully smoothing away
all the wrinkles, stocking the drawers
with clean T-shirts and socks.
In the kids' room she hides
her misshapen body under their beds.
Suddenly playful, she giggles, saying your name
with your children's voices, grabbing your feet
from under the bedspread.
Her hook-fingers get stuck on your clothes.

So you whisper her name, reel her in
to examine the scaly sheen of her body.
Her eyes fasten on yours and you're in a trance.
Everything falls to the side: the house,
its children, asleep in their beds,
the husband, who's never awake enough
to save you, anyway. You give way
to this wave of forgetting
as it slowly fills up your shoes.
When morning comes, you're a still
everglade, fathoms deep,
hiding a body that was, once, yours.

Mrs. Daley's Diamond Ring

Mrs. Daley had been waiting twenty-five years for a diamond ring from her husband. She was a quiet, humble woman who didn't ask for that much, though lately she found herself agitated and often yelling at Mr. Daley. She was human, after all, and wanted a few tokens of love and appreciation. He blamed her hormones.

Mr. Daley had proposed to her right after the war started, when he'd gotten a terrible draft number. To save money he'd planned to ask her to marry him in his own living room rather than go out but realized his father could have come in and disturbed them. Plus, whenever she visited, he noticed how filthy the place was. He couldn't propose at her house because her parents were always around, her mother making him dinner and sandwiches, especially BLTs, his favorite. And God knew he needed all the food he could get. It was embarrassing that he weighed less than the 118-pound girl he hoped to marry. With night school and his job washing glassware in a chemical company, he never seemed to find time to eat.

So they were sitting in the back of a bar they went to occasionally on Mount Auburn Street, each drinking a nickel beer. It was better proposing here, after all. You can't kneel when you're sitting in a booth, and the thought of kneeling did make Mike Daley feel a little silly.

He expected to be shipped out right after his medical, and he desperately wanted to marry Joan before he went. Mike reached into his pocket for the ring he'd bought her. It caught on a loose thread of the lining. She had to help him get it out. The salesman said he should buy the box, but it cost extra, and he didn't see the point of paying for something she'd never use. Engagement rings were kept on at all times. At least that's what the girl in the shop told him.

Although quite shy and very pleased at his proposal, the future Mrs.

Daley was not so overcome by the romance of the moment that she couldn't ask, "What kind of stone is this?" No one in her Italian family had much money, but all the women had some kind of diamond engagement ring, even if it was mixed with amethysts or garnets or other semi-precious stones. Rings were often passed down from older generations, but Joan didn't think, given the squalor Mike lived in, that anyone in his family had anything to pass down.

Mr. Daley smarted at her question. Lately he'd noticed nice-looking rings on her mother and her aunts, who visited frequently. His family rarely had callers. And no one had engagement rings. "It's a zircon." He looked down, his lips full, as they were back then when he was young and when Joan kissed them often. His slicked hair fell over his face, which he quickly combed back with his fingers. Mike looked at Joan expectantly. Surely the ring can't matter.

Joan sipped her beer quietly. She did love him, but her sisters had married Irishmen, and their marriages weren't working out well. Her mother was fond of Mr. Daley and impressed that he planned to spend eight years in night school to get a college degree. Joan liked the idea of a college boy. No one she knew had married one. Of course he could have gone to Harvard—taken that half scholarship he'd gotten—but his family couldn't afford the other half. Mr. Daley didn't feel bitter at this stage of his life because he wasn't used to getting anything easily, being poor and the youngest. But he did want his girl.

Perhaps he thought she might say no without the promise of some kind of diamond ring. Perhaps he imagined he'd be killed in the war. Who knows what went through his head, but Mr. Daley uncharacteristically burst out, "If you marry me now, I'll buy you a diamond for our twenty-fifth wedding anniversary." Joan thought this was the most endearing thing she'd ever heard. He was pledging his life to her. How could she refuse? Not to mention that in twenty-five years, they'd probably be able to afford quite a nice rock for her little hand. So they got married the next weekend, just in the rectory to save time and money. Joan said she could never have walked down the long aisle in church anyway, that she'd have fainted with nerves if everyone turned and stared at her.

Mr. Daley failed his medical because of his bad eyesight, flat feet, and low weight. But they just told people about his feet. Joan didn't want Mike to let on he was "suffering from malnutrition." Eventually Mr. Daley got his college degree and a decently paying job in an insurance company. They bought the two-family house he was living in when he met her. His father died and, after a dozen years or more, they had a daughter, Karen. Just the one. They saved up and bought a car. An Edsel, with that disastrous toilet-seat grill. The single most unpopular product in America. It got laughed at regularly, but Mr. Daley didn't mind because it was the cheapest used car in the lot. And they went on for a number of years without much change.

Though to Mrs. Daley, the word "zircon" gradually came to symbolize everything disappointing about their lives. Not just the Edsel, but that Mr. Daley, while making enough money, had no desire to move out of the two-family in Cambridge into a single in Belmont, a suburb one town over. That he begrudged her new clothes. Required detailed accounts of her spending. That he expected her to handle all the maintenance in the two-family—indoor painting, wallpaper, floor sanding, even basic plumbing. Mr. Daley hated the menial chores of property owning. Plus Mrs. Daley was good at working with her hands, and he believed she enjoyed it because she was Italian. Mrs. Daley would have preferred to have nicer hands and go to dances and out to dinner, but Mr. Daly had become quite the homebody. He enjoyed staying in with his wife and daughter. He did do much of the yard work on a Saturday, though. She had to give him that. And he didn't drink, except the occasional beer, and he never hit her.

Mrs. Daley learned to buy everything on sale and would always get seconds of any clothing she could find. Seconds were at least half price and often discounted more than that, and Mrs. Daley thought her husband particularly liked seconds because he'd always laugh and say he couldn't ever see flaws in them. And, of course, Mrs. Daley was busy raising their daughter, who made her so much happier than she'd ever been.

76

But lately she kept thinking how much closer they were to their twenty-fifth anniversary and that diamond ring. As angry as Mrs. Daley sometimes felt at Mr. Daley for not showing her enough love or gratitude, she never lost faith that the ring was on his mind almost as much as it was on hers, even though he always changed the subject when she mentioned it.

It seemed obvious to Karen, to Mrs. Daley's three sisters, and even to her mother that Mr. Daley never fully understood the promise he'd made to Joan. No one doubted he'd said it. Mrs. Daley didn't make things up, and she'd told her mother about it that very night. Her mother, frankly, found it odd then, but she wasn't one to interfere in her daughters' relationships. Joan had been a sickly child, but she'd grown into a fine-looking woman with a beautiful figure. So it was better all around to believe that Mike had meant what he'd said. And in the beginning, when she'd feed that young, handsome guy who came home late from college, his hands shaking from hunger, and only God knowing when the poor fellow had last eaten, you had to love him and believe a man that hardworking wouldn't disappoint Joan.

It was most painful during the last five years as Mrs. Daley counted down the time until Mr. Daley would buy her that ring. At every one of their anniversaries, she baked a delicious cake, frosted, and decorated it with buttercream icing. The yellow ring of roses adorning the top, with green leaves and vines—more elaborate every year—looked professionally created. Karen, who had little interest in baking, learned to use a pastry tube just so Mrs. Daley wouldn't feel alone on her anniversary and in her expectations.

When she was by herself, Mrs. Daley would sometimes stretch her left hand forward and wiggle her ring finger as if she could already see the diamond, sparkling in the sun. Mr. Daley's closest acknowledgment of his wife's desire was to compliment her baking, ask for another piece of the cake—though he was indifferent to the decorations—and give her a nice card. Mrs. Daley would put his card up for weeks by the Infant of Prague in the dining room, and she'd read it over and over.

Soon it was less than a month before their twenty-fifth anniversary,

77

and Mrs. Daley wondered if her husband hadn't mentioned the diamond because he planned to surprise her. But she suspected that was wishful thinking. So one evening during dinner, when Mr. Daley was thoroughly enjoying his steak and onions and the gravy Mrs. Daley had made especially for the potatoes she'd freshly mashed, she asked him directly. "Are you getting my ring on your own or do you want to shop for it together?"

Mr. Daley stared at her. Joan thought he looked like someone does when they get a wrong number. Nonetheless, she persisted. "I think we should go together, Mike, because I'd like to have some say, after all these years, in what the ring looks like."

Mr. Daley's Irish face turned quite red. "When do you propose we do this? After I come home from work? When will we eat? Or on the weekend when it's bedlam in town?" he snapped.

Mrs. Daley became as white as her husband was red and felt she could collapse with disappointment. She'd often told Karen that her father would give his daughter anything because "blood is thicker than water," while he denied his wife so much. Karen suddenly saw what her mother meant. Her father couldn't really fathom and didn't seem terribly interested in her mother's desires. Her mother's behavior had nothing to do with her hormones. Karen got up and rubbed her mother's shoulders. "Why don't Mom and I get the ring? I have more time than you, Daddy." Karen hadn't called him "Daddy" in years, and it stuck in her throat. "I love to shop." She sounded ridiculous, but he was more likely to agree if he felt superior to her. To them. Not cornered.

This wasn't what Mrs. Daley had been imagining. Her mind drifted back so easily to that night. Mr. Daley had been such a fine and earnest man. Now, with spittle in the corners of his narrow mouth, he was so changed.

Mr. Daley's body shook with fury. He hated diamonds with the way his wife went on and on about waiting for hers. How had she imagined he owed her one? Diamonds were the epitome of women's frivolous desires. They looked like clear glass, served no function, and were expensive. What woman would want one other than to prove she could manipulate a man into buying something completely useless? Why had Mrs. Daley nagged him for twenty-five years about this damn ring, never giving it a rest?

Mrs. Daley started to cry. "How 'bout it, Dad?" Karen smiled warmly at him, her voice happy and cajoling.

Mr. Daley grimaced. "All right. But it better not be expensive. She's gone all this time without one. I hardly see the point." Mr. Daley talked as if Mrs. Daley weren't in the room.

Karen and her mother discovered a rather enormous diamond in an estate jewelry store. The ring was cut, the salesman explained, in an intricate style that caught every light. "Stonecutters haven't the skill to create a diamond like this today." Mrs. Daley touched the ring and her lip trembled. Karen explained that her mother had waited twenty-five years and felt afraid to ask the price because her father was a thrifty man. After a while, when Mrs. Daley kept refusing to try on the ring, Karen saw the jeweler pull off the price tag and toss it aside.

"Let's just see how it looks," he said gently.

"H-how much?" Karen's mother whispered, letting him pick up her rough hand and slide the ring on.

Karen walked around the counter and peered at the tiny price tag— $3000.

The salesman shook his head. "Just two thousand dollars."

"Why?" Mrs. Daley asked, taking off the ring. She thought diamonds were much more expensive.

"Two reasons," he said matter-of-factly, inspecting the ring through his jeweler's monocle. "Given its crown, the stone needs a deeper pavilion." Noticing Mrs. Daley's confusion, he explained that the bottom half of the diamond was too small for its top. She nodded. He readjusted the monocle and sighed. "Then there's the fact that the stone itself is flawed. A yellow spot right at the point."

Mrs. Daley asked how obvious the spot was. She hadn't noticed it.

"It's not visible to the naked eye," the jeweler smiled. "But perhaps it's why the diamond has so little depth. The cutter probably didn't see the defect until late in his work and salvaged the stone by eliminating as much of the flaw as possible. Were this stone deeper and pure, the ring would cost over five thousand dollars."

Mrs. Daley began to smile.

The salesman expected, when he took off his monocle, to find Mrs. Daley disheartened. No one who'd waited twenty-five years would want a diamond that was doubly flawed. But far from being disappointed, Mrs. Daley, grasping Karen's hands, exclaimed, "It's a Godsend. We can tell him we found a ring that's a 'second.' And less than half price." The salesman was shocked. But neither Karen nor her mother noticed. He agreed to hold the ring for three days.

When they told Mr. Daley about the ring that night—Mrs. Daley emphasizing all the while that it was a "second," and a great buy—Mr. Daley said that $2000 was an outrageous amount to spend all at once. He banged his fork on his plate and reminded Mrs. Daley and Karen that he'd grown up in poverty and that neither of them brought in one cent to the household. That every responsibility—the house, Karen's education at the Catholic school, the food they ate, the clothes they wore, the telephone they talked on, the furniture, the dishes, the fence, everything—was all his. That it was outrageous to spend $2000 when the only reason they had any money was because every week he saved something from his paltry paycheck. Mr. Daley stormed out of the room, saying he'd had enough. That there would be no diamond.

Mr. and Mrs. Daley fought all night. Karen heard her mother repeating, "Two thousand dollars for twenty-five years! Not even a hundred dollars a year. Am I really worth so little to you?" By the morning they weren't speaking to each other. After school Karen and her mother went back to the store. Karen begged the salesman to reduce the price, explaining her father's position. He looked from one of them to the other and appeared genuinely moved, then lowered the price to $1700.

Mr. Daley had no choice but to see the ring. He told the salesman that diamonds meant nothing to him. "Why would anyone wear diamonds unless they're trying to show off or behave like they're rich when they're not?" He taunted. But the jeweler didn't answer Mr. Daley's questions, so they couldn't get into an argument. He remained composed and kept saying the most pleasant things.

"A wise investment."

"Your lovely wife and daughter."

"An incredible deal."

He was kind, even tender.

"A ring a man can be proud to have bought his wife."

He sounded like he could reassure them forever.

"Twenty-five years…it's as if there's a facet for every loving moment you've had together." Mrs. Daley gave him a look for that line.

Eventually Mr. Daley had to give in and buy Mrs. Daley the ring.

"Would you like to wear it now?" the salesman asked.

Mrs. Daley's eyes sparkled almost as much as the ring.

"Don't be ridiculous," Mr. Daley sneered. "We take the train. She's not wearing a diamond on the subway. Perfect place for a mugging." The box was included with this ring, and Mr. Daley shoved it into his inside jacket pocket, where it would be relatively safe.

When they got home Mrs. Daley asked Mike for the ring, hoping he might want to put it on her himself, as he had long ago with the zircon. She smiled her best smile. "Well, Mike, at least it's not caught on a thread in your pocket," she said, trying to help him remember. But he tossed the box onto the dining room table.

Mrs. Daley pushed the ring down her dry, chapped finger. She went to the kitchen window to wiggle her hand in the sunlight. The diamond's reflections danced around the room, and Mrs. Daley thought of how shocked her sisters would be when they saw her gorgeous diamond. The twenty-five-year wait was worth it after all.

But Mr. Daley pushed her back from the window. "Don't flash that ring outside, advertising to strangers that we have things worth stealing in our house." She covered the diamond with her right hand. "There's only one way you're keeping that ring, and it isn't in our house. It goes into the safety deposit box at the bank on Monday or it goes back to the store." Mrs. Daley asked him if he meant they'd do this until the ring was insured. But Mr. Daley unconditionally refused to insure it, saying he'd already spent quite enough money. He warned his wife of the serious financial loss they'd sustain were the diamond to be stolen. Mrs. Daley pleaded with him to call the insurance company, just to get a figure. Mr. Daley would not. She had wanted a "priceless gem." This was the consequence of her wishes. So the ring went to and remained in the safe deposit box.

Years later, when Karen finished her schooling and had a secure job, she offered to insure the ring. Mr. Daley would have none of that, so he finally did it himself. The ring was then worth $8,000. Karen knew there was no point noting what a good financial investment the diamond was.

Karen drove her mother to the bank for the ring. She slipped it over her mother's arthritic knuckle in the car, and Mrs. Daley made pleasant little sounds as she fondled the ring and watched it sparkle all the way home. When they got back, Mrs. Daley cried a little and thanked Karen, who made them a pot of tea and offered to clean the ring so it shone all the more. Her mother looked so happy. It was just such a shame that her sisters, who'd died many years before, had never gotten to see it.

Karen went out to see an old friend for an hour or so and came back to find pairs of her mother's gloves all over the kitchen table, her father seething, and her mother trembling. "Well, get used to it!" he was shouting. For an old man, Mr. Daley still fought as if he were in his prime. But nowadays Mrs. Daley couldn't handle arguments. Her blood pressure went up, her nose bled, and she needed to lie down. Karen helped her into bed. Apparently Mr. Daley had yelled at his wife, insisting that she'd need to put on gloves whenever she wore the damn ring outside the house. And he'd obviously further upset her by criticizing Karen's interference.

But when she got up, Mrs. Daley attitude had changed. She realized now what a mistake she'd made. When anyone saw it on her—and how could they not, the way it glistened—they'd assume she and Mr. Daley were wealthy. Their house would be burgled, and it would be her fault.

And then where would she and Mr. Daley be?

So, although the ring was insured, it had to go back into the safe deposit box. Mr. Daley bought Mrs. Daley a new zircon on sale for $75. And Joan told Karen on the phone later that week that her nerves were finally calmed to have that diamond out of the house.

Blood and Diamonds

Now: Blood, drying in the sun,
    on the back of an old man's neck

    Next: Diamonds, circling a newly-perfect
    neck, dazzling the eyes of marginal dreamers

    Again: Blood, dripping from a boy-child's
    fly-filled ear

    Forward: Perfume ad: a sculpted bottle of tiny,
    sparkling diamonds, tossed between carefree,
    genderless hands

2

        The substantial, deep-voiced spectre in substantial
        robes, Christmas Carol robes, Christmas-Present robes,
        parts them to reveal small, shoeless, bug-eyed,
        open-mouthed beings, knees to their chests, squinting
        in unsubdued light.

 The spectre speaks:

    "This boy is Ignorance, this girl is Want. Beware of them both,
but most
    of all beware this boy, for on his brow I see that written which is
Doom,
    unless the writing be erased ...."

Scrooge cries out:

"Have they no refuge or resource?"

The spectre mocks him:

"Are there no prisons? Are there no workhouses?"

3

Young, rich, wired -
the new millennium speaks:

> Keep those stock prices up, baby,
> keep those designer jeans-tees-
> earrings-drugs coming.
>
> Profit's an old man's game,
> dealing Blue Chips, tearing up
> over widows and orphans. You really
> think they cared? Did you?
>
> It's our time, now, big-time, easy time;
> everyone's making it to the top.
>
> Poverty? What poverty? Where? That garbage
> mountain crushing those people? All that smoking
> filth. And blood - that stench of drying blood -
> hey - they said that's in the Philippines. What
> do we have to do with them? A million years ago,
> maybe - who was it, again - McCarthy? McArthur?
> Somebody - not us, baby.
>
> Here? You mean poverty here? I suppose ...

in Appalachia, maybe - or is it the Adirondacks?
Where Ever it is. Don't sidetrack me here ...

And don't show me those pictures, again - they're
nauseating - how can people live like that?
That old man should take a shower and that kid's
mother should be given a talking-to.
They're animals. Those people.

And we're the top.
So we scramble for diamonds - so what?
So those diamonds are scattered by
the Invisible Man - so what?

Who the hell are you?
So you sold your soul for less;
so you can sleep at night.
So can I.

So can I So can I So can I So   can   I

Elijah

They named him Elijah, gave him his line for entering a room: *Is it me you are waiting for?* In the Bible, a vortex of twisted wind takes Elijah to heaven—and he appears again, talking to Jesus, at Jesus's transfiguration. "Where you been?" they ask each other. The answer is obvious: "Hanging around."

Elijah hangs around outside my classroom with the three prettiest girls in twelfth grade, thin, wispy girls like supermodels. I play dumb, keep asking him how a guy like him gets to hang out with this bevy of beauties, as if I don't know the answer to that one. Gay Elijah. Talk about suffering. Being gay in high school. Christ.

He comes out to me the last day of his senior year, right after finals.

"Is it me you are waiting for?" he says. Elijah looks like a politician, with short-cropped hair and buttoned-up shirts and a perpetual handout ready for shaking. I hate his dry hands; they remind me of how wet mine always are.

"What's up, soon-to-be graduate?"

"I'm gay," he says. "Just thought I should tell you, you know, you always asking about the girls."

Student confessions. One writes at the bottom of her essay, "By the way, my brother raped me. Don't tell anyone." Instead of a pencil, another puts a one-hitter on his desk. Another tells me not to schedule the conference because her mom will show up high. All of them lead to notes to the guidance counselor, sessions, calls, meetings. But what about being gay? What does that warrant these days?

"My parents know," he says, "so don't worry."

"So what do you want me to do, Elijah?"

"Nothing. I just want to tell you."

"That's it. Just tell me."

"Jesus, Mr. Brown. Doesn't anyone just tell you things?"

"Just for the heck of it?"

"Yeah. Just for the heck of it."

"No," I say. "Not just for the heck of it."

" Do you want to do anything? Is that it? You inherited that fix-it gene?"

"Do you want fixed?"

"Do I want fixed? They told me I shouldn't tell you anything. I thought you were cool."

"See. You did want something, didn't you? What? What is it? When you pictured this moment, what did I say after you confessed?"

"You said, 'That's cool.'"

"Okay," I say. "So why don't you go out and come back in. Tell me. And I'll say exactly that."

"And that will mean what?"

"Well my thought was that you would want me to treat it as nothing, like you told me you were wearing a new shirt. That would show me to be cool about it, that it doesn't change a thing. Only I was wrong. I blew it. So I want a second chance, okay?"

"*You* want a second chance?"

Elijah walks out of the classroom, shuts the door but it bounces off the door frame and remains open a crack. I sit across from the empty seat, wait for his return.

88

Finding the Father Grave, June 19

Follow route 50 east from any inner harbors.
Pass the corn and cabbage fields, long tables of fruit.
Churches and shoulder-side shacks, all the goings-on within.
Don't think of the long trip back.

Pretend until pretending becomes praise.
The house: an attic stuffed with steamer-trunks
stuffed with photographs. A boy—yellow slicker
sleeves rolled high against a blue-black storm.

Innocent, you who still suppose such things,
of the forward-backward game of desolation or hope.
Go to the kitchen. He's there, has been for sometime.
Think of the long conversation.

How he sweltered all that summer. Told a few jokes.
Loved a woman. Tired mouths suspended,
whiskey-stopped. Silence. "No," you'd say,
"I won't be staying on tonight."

Reminders in the rear-view mirror. A tuft of hair; the brow.
Take the stone turn off, hardly a car's width wide.
Everything's been arranged. Habitual Flowers,
a new plastic breed. The same exotic orchids.

In among the quenched lanterns, moss-eaten
lambs fed fat on sun and rain, fifty or so speaking-stones.
One speaks a familiar name. Cross-legged, buttocks pressing
queerly into the ground, admit now why you've come.

Dement, It

If my skin was tighter I could keep the cold out. When I lift my neck and head upwards, even an inch, I find my worn skin becomes prickly with chills. Assisted living brings us to the beach every Friday in the summer. I hate the beach and the breeze that swirls above the ocean.

"Catch," some no face kid yells a few feet from me. I clench my butt cheeks and hope they don't trip on me; but of course, they land right on my back, elbow driving into my spine.

I jerk up and am punctured by cold air, harsher than an elbow to the back. A gurgle comes from my throat.

I rub my right wrist that was jammed into the ground, kneading the kinks out of my faded Dennis the Menace tattoo. When I look up the kid is pulling herself out of the sand.

She's hardly a kid; she's as beautiful as Deb O'Brien was the day I didn't kiss her, when she let me walk her home from a piano lesson. The freckles that splatter her face are painted in the same pattern as my old dreamboat.

"I'm sorry, sir. My boyfriend tripped me," she said.

"Which one of these punks is your boyfriend?" I want to kiss her.

I catch her staring at the drooping under my eyes.

"The one with the buzz cut, walking away, hand in the waistband of his trunks," she replied.

I'm 70 years too late to kiss her.

"Damn kid."

She giggles.

"Did I say that out loud?"

"Yes, you did." Her delicate hands brush down her body and she stretches her black swim bottoms to cover her entire butt. Sand floats to the ground "Is there anything I can do to help you? Where's your family?"

"Not everyone has one of those."

Caught off guard, she gives a soft apology.

She is deliberate and respectful with her word choice, but her tone screams infancy. I can handle the baby talk. *Kiss me.* She grabs my hand and I crawl up her arm and stand. It isn't until I am close up, face to face; that I realize that it's *her.*

"Can I kiss you, Deb?"

"Excuse me?"

Her sequined black bikini, now a calf-length polka dotted dress twisting around her form in the breeze that hit like a knuckle sandwich. I'm staring at her ankles, gorgeous ankles. I can feel my skin tighten and hair thicken and curl in a youthful return. I am a twig again.

"Please, Deb."

"My name isn't Deb, I'm Morgan."

She fills out the dress just the way that she should.

A cloud is filling my chest, rejection seeping in. I want to run my fingers through that thick red hair and kiss her, reclaim what is mine.

"I need to go get you some help."

"I have to kiss ya, babe. I've been waiting too long." I lean in and grab her face. At the same time her hands reach for my shoulders and I'm suddenly tipping like a domino to the ground, face first in the sand. It's so warm, I just want to wrap myself in my towel and let our creases become one. Bruises are already forming on both shoulders.

By the time I look up, sand has crusted in my broom-brittle mustache. I see the baldhead coming back my direction and Deb is repeating how sorry she is.

"Is it because I didn't go to war like James did?" I spit out bits of sand between each word.

Deb is no longer facing me. She had her hands all over baldhead and I could feel the tension between them. She was dying to kiss him.

"Honey, no, it's ok." Baldhead did not look like James. "I think he's having trouble telling where he is. It's kind of cute."

Kiss her. Get back up and kiss her. That mantra was pounding so hard in my head that I didn't hear what baldhead had to say.

91

I couldn't stand fast enough before they walked away. Kiss her. She was looking back at me, red lipstick curling up in a sad smile.

Sharp bits of seashells stab my feet as I walk up to the small waves that plaster the shoreline. My skin shrivels up. I want to take in the ocean, let it rejuvenate me; but there is no escaping it. There is no such thing as the fountain of youth and there is a nurse running towards me.

Time is Money

It was barter at first.
The waves rose frothing toward
the shore, like generations spilling
novelty into each new indifferent decade,
spreading out into infinite flattened sand
to receive them and to watch their conquest
chase small crabs up to a high-water mark,
which was an evident give while the subtle take
disappeared invisibly into the undertow,
or matched each wave by molecule with
an equal feint and yield of salt sea air.
Nothing was lost.

Hoarding time was a hubris of the empires.
Four thousand head-shaven Taoist monks
sat motionless in a giant mountain cave,
counting out only shared exhalations into
windless echoing air and common darkness,
storing up such a fortune of empty minutes
that death itself would have to forfeit all keys
to its eternity hidden behind the far polar star
if frozen-faced comrades in combat fatigues
had not lurched in to douse them all in gasoline,
rousing the very red mountain dragon's wrath
whose fire had swallowed empires long before.

Stealing time fails, too, in any bid to reallocate,
yet often not before forty towering fortresses

93

have been built to shackle victims of the theft,
doing time as thieves lose all track of their spoils
and as hours stiffen into gridlock that opens cracks
in concrete cellblock walls wide enough at first
for only grass blades, then for ants in single file,
then for a rat, and at last for a human hand and foot,
a living jailbreak from death that was not waited for
until time to waste or spend at last can be restored.

Investing time would seem to hold a greater promise.
Beeswax builds in tongue-smoothed spittled layers,
a pixilation of hexagons to house a humming brood,
abuzz with frenzied wings and waggled chatter over
orientation to a universe of bright surrounding bloom,
layer upon layer of dark distilled gold summer light,

all stored against the snows that can freeze a single bee
or shrink cities of its kin down to stragglers into spring,
if not first crushed by clawed, thickened paws of bears,
out to plunder honey and fat for their own deep snores
in dark dens they have discovered but rarely ever built.

What of saving time, the cultivation of its thrift?
A windswept heron sways on a branch of juniper,
the spindles of his avian leather legs locked stiff,
his beak spear poised above choppy shaded water,
his eye beaded at what stirs below its surface light,
and his coils of neck looping gently out and back,
the only movement spent in all his hours of wait.
Or ospreys, too, surveying seas from wings locked
tight for sky rides high on stiff incoming winds,
sparing breath for beak dives down to the waves.
Not to mention the patient plants, trees that nod
into every breeze and stand through every night,

94

fingering countless threaded roots through soil
in shade while lifting only green up into light.

But the giving of time alone is what is everything,
as nature gives from its reserves of time so generous,
so inky deep beyond reckoning that digits we derive
from fingers must nest inside each other just to keep
from shrinking to a dust or being blown from off the page,
so beyond our grasp its cycles loop to suckle us to its skies:
Our nights fill up with beetle chirps and breezes off the sea,
our mornings rise to follow shadow like the shy and slender
deer,
our days of honeysuckle never tire of scenting air with bloom,
while empty shells make tiny chevrons out of thin receding tide,
and sunset shimmers brightly off of glistening sheets of sand.
The wind flings endless buffetings at bracken on the shore,
and dashes apart a thousand wave crests without cause.
The ocean stirs beyond the rim of anything we see,
and heaves itself like frothing stallions surging
over and over and over against the shore.
The open sky is vast, the waters wide.
The hours gallop only when we ride.

The Philosopher

A stranger to the desert, a philosopher from one of the great cities on the continent to the north heard of this oasis and undertook preparations to travel. He was an admired and respected man, and he possessed in himself all the best virtues of his people. He was systematic in his thought, receptive to new ideas, generous of spirit. But despite these attributes, the body flagged even as his mind excelled. The philosopher determined to sojourn to the oasis because he had heard of its healing waters and although he did not fear death, he still believed he had more work to do. Of course, rumors of the desert water's healing powers ran rampant in the north; the people of the desert knew the sad inaccuracy of these tales, for they had bathed in those waters for thousands of years and still they watched their loved ones die from the failings of the body. Nevertheless, all the credible sources to the philosopher's ear extolled their healing powers—or perhaps the philosopher merely assigned his faith where he wanted, for when days are days of exhaustion and pain, even the greatest minds seek comfort—and he sailed to the mouth of the desert, where he loaded a camel with supplies and bowed his head to the wind blowing across the sands.

The pace of his journey's beginning was no slower than anticipated, and steady. By nightfall of the tenth day however, he could no longer control his fear. He sat on a carpet in front of his camel-dung fire and, in the sand, he redrew the map of the land from memory. A five day journey for a young man in good health, the philosopher had reasonably allotted to himself ten days, had hoped for eight or nine. He had yet, in all his time in the desert, to see another wanderer, although he could find little reason for the inhabitants of this place to stray far from their city and its water. The water sprang four days south and one day east of the port on the sea. Was it possible he had turned east too early? By what arrogance had he not first followed the coast? He had supplies for twenty days. If he turned back now, he would leave the desert only as alive as he had entered it, succumbing to the body. The philosopher snatched the robes about his attenuated chest. He had been made old, not by the revolutions of the seasons, but by the deficiencies of the flesh. He cursed his wretched body, but knew that when the sun rose upon the sands, he would continue south towards the oasis.

By the fourteenth day, traveling south, then further east, then south some more, the philosopher, a calm and reasonable mind, felt the unfamiliar fluttering of panic in his breast. He trekked west; perhaps he had gone too far east instead of south. He trekked north. On the nineteenth day, supplies dwindling, he dropped the camel's rope and stood still. Reason is indistinguishable from madness in the desert. Facing north, towards his homeland, the philosopher raised his right forearm to his forehead—to block the sun?—and resolved to stand still, to expend as little energy as possible, to hope for rescue. On the first day, the sun turned his shoulder to stone. When night fell, the philosopher tried to lower his arm and found that he could not. He looked down and saw the stony skin. He reached across with his left hand and felt his shoulder: the hard, rough grain of sandstone. He dropped back his left arm, lest it too turn to stone. On the second day, the stone weight of his left ankle sank into the sand. Each day, the sun turned another patch of skin to stone. But the philosopher did not die; the stone kept him alive. A triage on the living body, limbs and non-essential organs ossified first. When the sluggish blood could no longer feed the hungry brain, his head hardened, his last thoughts on the immortality of the immaterial soul. Only the chest remained alive, the attenuated chest. The blood pooled in the chambers of the heart and it beats still, a statue of living flesh.

Shadow Box: A Ghazal

"Tattoos and Body Piercings" read the neon sign on the wall.
Her shadow ducked and trembled, a quivering line on the wall.

When the Earth's plates converged, time held its breath—for a second.
Then the grandfather clock stumbled, smearing eight and nine on the
wall.

The phone call arrived during dinner. Fate's message wrapped inside
a gasp, a broken glass, and a splatter of wine on the wall.

The garden lay overgrown. Weeds choked the gutters. The deck sagged.
Birds, flying overhead, dropped gum wrappers and twine on the wall.

Twenty red lights, six jammed lanes, and two cups of coffee later,
he shuffled to his cubicle and hung his spine on the wall.

Dust mites littered the living room, except for the mantle which held
a shiny urn and two tapered candles: a shrine on the wall.

Stop, drop, and roll isn't always the best exit plan so she
buried her pennies and planted a climbing vine on the wall.

Right before he took that nasty spill (he was pushed, rumors claim,)
Humpty-Dumpty (a spy, by accounts) looked divine on the wall.

She wore coral in her hair, bright as the sea, and the waves
flowing through her veins made her spirit shine on the wall.

Risk

Carol lifted her last yellow army from the board, relieved Peter had beaten her. He could be such a jackass when he lost.

Peter picked up the challenger dice and pointed at the board. "Your turn, Drew. Kamchatka to Irkutsk." He was wearing a t-shirt that said *FUXXUP*, in Exxon's red and blue, across the white cotton.

"Hang in there, Drew. You're the last bastion against the sweeping black hoard." Lily swallowed the rest of her wine and refilled her glass.

Peter rolled the dice between his hands. "Hey, Lily, how about a little wifely support? Drew's got about as much chance of winning as Reagan does of getting those Star Wars lasers hitting anything."

Lily set the bottle on the table so hard it wobbled.

Peter grabbed the neck of the bottle. "Steady, hon. Don't be a sore loser."

"I'm not." She shoved back from the table. "Come on, Carol. Let the boys battle it out." She leaned over to gather empty bottles and glasses. Her short shorts rode up.

Peter ran his finger across the crescent of pale skin at the top of her thigh. "Hey, bring me another beer, babe."

"You know where it is, hon." Lily slapped his hand away and tugged at her shorts.

Carol stood up and grabbed the chip bowl. If Peter and Lily were going to start sniping at each other again, she didn't want to be here. She touched Drew's shoulder, but he kept studying the board.

In the kitchen, Lily held the bottle out. "I hate Risk. Peter always wins and he's so damn smug about it."

"Games are more than games to him. I dreaded being his bridge partner. Remember that time I miscounted trump?" Peter had slammed his hand on the table and knocked over his beer.

"Yeah, he can be pretty unforgiving." Lily opened the refrigerator.

"Shit. We're out of beer. He was supposed to pick some up." She grabbed her shoulder bag and called out, "Beer run."

Peter's voice, "Come on, baby." Dice hit the tabletop.

Lily backed the truck out of the driveway fast, barely missing the mailbox. She turned a knob. Clashing cymbals and jangled guitars assaulted Carol's chest. The words were lost in the blare. Lily's finger jabbed a button. "Give me a break." The tape ejected and she tossed it on the seat between them.

Carol rubbed the spot above her right eye where her headaches started. "What was that?"

"Iron Maiden. Peter's latest love. I'll take James Taylor and Carole King any day." Lily hummed the beginning of "Fire and Rain." There were crow's feet at the corners of her eyes Carol had never noticed before. Taking the curves one-handed, she punched in the cigarette lighter. "You ever wonder why Peter and Drew are still friends?"

Carol opened Lily's purse and rooted around for the Marlboros, lit two, put one in Lily's mouth. "Games. Gadgets. Soccer." Drew had been so happy when Peter suggested forming a team, recreating high school glory days. She'd met Lily at a game, both of them pacing the sidelines to keep warm.

Lily inhaled. "Does Drew go to strip clubs?"

"I don't think so. It's never come up. Why? Does Peter?"

"Sometimes." Lily lifted her long hair off her nape. "God, it's so fucking hot. Why can't he like short hair?"

From the day they met, Lily had measured out her sharing like the ingredients of a secret recipe. She would tell Carol what she wanted to. There was no point in pushing her. "Drew and I got this really cheap flight to Paris when we were in grad school. We went to a strip club on the Right Bank. We only had enough money for one drink so we stood at the rail and nursed a cognac for hours. I got bored."

"You're the only person I know who'd get bored at a strip show."

"The acts weren't what I expected. Stagey. I thought it would be a turn-on, that we'd go back to our hotel room and, you know."

"Screw like rabbits?"

The women had looked like mannequins, their faces smooth masks, their lips red. The last act was two women. They stroked each others' gleaming bodies, intertwined, their eyes closed. It was the only act that turned her on. She hadn't told Drew that.

Lily pulled into the Albertson's parking lot. "What did Drew think?"

"He said it was interesting."

"His favorite word. Funny, what does and doesn't turn you on."

They hadn't made love that night. Drew had spooned against her, run his hand over her hip, and she had edged away. Carol's cigarette tasted charred. She stubbed it out.

Lily twisted her cigarette in the ashtray. "Are you coming to the game?"

"Miss the first game of the season?" Another autumn of Saturday mornings sitting on the sidelines freezing. She'd never liked soccer, just another team chasing a ball.

~ ~ ~

Lily threw her purse and keys on the counter. "We're back." From the living room, loud laughter, canned. "Oh, God, that fucking channel."

"What?"

"Playboy. Their version of Candid Camera. Tits and ass."

Peter ambled into the kitchen. "Did you get some munchies?" He stretched and his t-shirt slid up exposing dark belly hair. He scratched at his navel. He was getting a beer belly.

"Just beer. For which you could thank me. The A/C's not working in the truck, remember?"

"I suppose that's my fault, too."

Carol went to the sink and rinsed out her glass. The sun beat through the bay window above the kitchen sink. The plants needed water. Even the succulents looked parched.

Peter shoved things around on the counter, knocked over the salt shaker. White grains scattered. "Where's the church key?"

Lily opened a drawer and tossed him the opener. "You were supposed to take the truck in, remember?" She refilled her glass. Wine splattered on the counter.

Peter flipped the cap off and chugged the Killian's Red. Drops clung to his mustache. He wiped it with the back of his hand. "And I worked overtime three days this week." He was cultivating a Tom Selleck mustache. He was addicted to *Magnum, P.I.,* said he'd always wanted to live in Hawaii and spend all his free time on the beach.

Lily threw the church key back in the drawer and slammed it shut. "Right."

"What's that supposed to mean?"

"You know what it means. Just tell me the girls didn't come up and see that crap."

Peter took another gulp. "They're still downstairs. Haven't heard a peep."

"And that's a good sign?" Lily put the beer in the refrigerator. "I'm going to check on them."

Peter watched her go. "Christ, she's touchy. That time of the month?"

"I wouldn't know." She hated how quickly his needling got her off-balance.

"Don't you women talk about these things?"

"We women don't call each other up every month, if that's what you mean."

He put his hands up, palms toward her. "Whoa, Carol. Just kidding."

She turned away. Her headache was worse.

In the living room, the TV was off. Drew was sitting back at the table, scooping blue armies off the board. He grinned up at her. "I beat him."

"We need to go."

~~~

In the car, she turned the A/C vent so the cool air blew right on her face and closed her eyes.

Drew rested his hand on her thigh. "Were they fighting again?"

"What do you think?" She tapped a cigarette out of the pack and lit

102

it. Her heart sped up with the rush. "Want one?"

He shook his head. "Christ. They're always at each other."

"She asked me if you went to strip clubs."

He moved his hand to the wheel. "Out of the blue?"

"She said Peter goes sometimes." She touched his cheek. Blond stubble grazed her fingertips. "What if you tried talking to him?"

"Pete doesn't talk about personal stuff." He accelerated, shifted into third. He always let the stick rest for a second in neutral. "They're our best friends."

She studied the end of her cigarette. Best friends. Wisps of blue-grey smoke floated up. She should ask him right out if he'd ever gone to a strip club.

Drew pulled into the driveway and shut the car off. "Lily's parents have never liked him."

"What does that have to do with it?"

"I don't know, Carol." Drew shoved his glasses up and massaged his eyes. "It just seems like she's mad at Pete all the time."

Drew had known him for twenty years. She shouldn't have to tell him what a jackass Peter could be.

~~~

Lily sipped her drink. She'd eaten the cherry as soon as the bartender put the glass in front of her. "Give me a Manhattan any day. Who'd want to drink something called a Fuzzy Navel? What's in it anyway?"

"Peach brandy, I think." Carol wished she'd ordered a coke instead of a Harvey Wallbanger. It had been a long day at work. The first twinge pinged above her right eye. She wouldn't have agreed to meet Lily for happy hour if that undercurrent hadn't been in her voice. They'd been sitting here half an hour, Lily was on her second drink, had moved from a rant about undependable volunteers to an A-Z list of Peter's faults. Carol pushed her glass away. "Lily, I need to get to the store."

Lily stirred her drink with the plastic sword from the cherry. "There's this guy at work. He asked me to have a drink with him."

"What did you tell him?" Carol split the red and white straw with

103

her thumbnail.

"That I was having a drink with you." Lily lit a cigarette.

"Clever you."

"He's going to ask again."

The pain behind Carol's eye spread. "And you're going to say no."

"I'm not so sure. He's just so nice, so fucking nice."

"Lily." Carol touched her arm.

Lily pulled away. "Don't you dare judge me, Carol. You got one of the good ones. Remember when I asked you if Drew went to strip clubs?" Lily's voice was harsh as gravel under tires. "Peter goes every Friday with his buddies from Nam. Shoving money we don't have in some bimbo's G-string. One time, he says to me, 'Listen, Lily, you never take crisp bills to a strip joint. It's uncomfortable for the lovely ladies, paper cuts y'know'. His exact words." Her laugh was red and ugly.

"Please don't do anything stupid."

"He didn't even make it to the hospital the night Jessica was born. Appears the next day with an armload of roses, shit-eating grin on his face. Fucking bastard." Lily inhaled as if she were going to smoke the cigarette in one breath.

Orange juice and Galliano rose in Carol's throat. She swallowed hard.

"I shouldn't have told you." Lily put her cigarettes and lighter in her purse. "Promise me you won't tell Drew."

Drew would think Lily was exaggerating. "I promise."

~~~

"What did Lily want?" Drew uncapped a beer.

"Just to bitch." She squeezed the teabag against her spoon.

"About Peter?"

"I promised her I wouldn't tell you." The headache thumped behind her eye. What was she thinking? He'd worry it like a terrier now, and he was loyal to the point of blindness where Peter was concerned.

"Don't you want to help them?"

She sipped her tea. "How is my telling you going to help them?"

104

She didn't really like chamomile, but it was supposed to be soothing. "Have you ever been to a strip club?"

"What does that have to do with anything?"

"I just want to know."

He tilted the bottle and swallowed. "A couple of times. Some of the guys go after work."

Tassels swirling on perfect melon breasts. She saw his hand reaching out, stuffing bills in a sequined G-string, the belly above it flat and taut.

"It doesn't mean anything, Carol. It's just something guys do." He set the empty bottle down hard. "I just wish you'd tell me what she said."

"I can't."

"You mean you won't." Drew rubbed at the ring the beer bottle had left on the table. "I'm going for a walk."

She stood at the kitchen window smoking, watching the dark come down. The desert sky was that milky color that had no name.

Drew came back, went in the study and shut the door. She kept filling her glass till the bottle was empty and it was late enough for bed.

All that week, she and Drew spoke the short, practical sentences of everyday.

~~~

The grass on the sidelines was wet. The sun burned through an early morning fog, but the air was chilly. She scanned the onlookers. No Lily. Arms across each others' backs, heads down, Peter and Drew huddled with the rest of the team. Drew's blue goalie shirt stood out from all the black shirts.

Lily walked up, a beach chair under each arm. She wasn't wearing makeup. Her lips were chalky.

Carol took one of the chairs. "Where are the girls?"

"They stayed overnight at a friend's." Lily opened her bag and pulled out her cigarettes. She flicked the lighter. Her hands were shaking. "It's freezing out here."

Carol took the lighter and Lily leaned in, inhaled.

105

The ref blew the whistle and the two teams ran out onto the field. He set the ball on the grass and flipped a coin, a glint of silver in the sun. He looked at the back of his hand and pointed at Peter. The defenders positioned themselves, Peter ran forward and took the first kick, and they were away down the field. A flash of bare, muscled calves and the other team's fullback had the ball. Drew crouched in the cage, caught up in a world she didn't care about. He yelled something she couldn't hear and Peter flipped him the bird.

Lily laughed. "The same dance every season." She put her head back and closed her eyes. "I had a drink with the guy at work. It was so easy, talking to him. He felt it, too, said he hadn't felt so comfortable with someone in a long time."

"You barely know him, Lily. He's new, mysterious." All that rush of discovery, that chance to be new yourself, to start over with someone who didn't know the worst about you.

Lily rubbed the back of her neck. Her hair was up in a ponytail. "I'm so tired of being unhappy."

"What about the girls?"

"If we split up? They'd survive. Most of their friends' parents are divorced."

Carol's world tilted. "You could try talking to someone."

"Peter wouldn't go. He doesn't believe in showing your dirty linen. Besides, you know what they say about marriage counseling. By the time you try it, it's too late." Lily rubbed her arms. "Christ, it's cold." She stood up. "I've got to go. I'll call you." She walked away.

On the field, the other team's forward took a pass and kicked toward the far side of the net. Drew leaped in the air, a blur of blue, his body arched. His forearms connected with the ball and drove it away from the goal. He leaped again, arms shooting up, fists punching the sky. When the ball hit the ground, Peter was there. His kick drove the ball down the field. Drew cupped his hands around his mouth and yelled, "Go, Pete." It was what he always said.

106

Reality Show

The baby cries

a cat scurries

the dog appears

the baby sleeps

(what joy is this

says the mouse

to the cheese)

between sheets

the lovers lie

to each other

their rage is vast

& endless

what fresh hell is this

(you talkin' to me?)

the dog barks

the lovers' cries

are borrowed

from The Young

and The Restless

My American Dream

Whatever your daughter tells you about when she started having sex, assume it's a lie. That's my advice, and you can ignore it at your peril. Your sweet little girl, the apple of your eye, started screwing a lot earlier than she'll admit, guaranteed. And when my own daughter said to me, "It's none of your fucking business, but just so you'll stop asking, Ronnie's my first," I knew she was lying. And I smacked her across the face.

"Darlene, you're a liar," I said, and I wasn't thinking, I just smacked her, and it is a moment that I will regret for the rest of my life. I wished I could cut off my hand, sever the offending limb, the guilt I felt immediately while the feel of her cheek still burned on my palm.

Her face showed a hundred emotions, none of them good, none of them what the Dalai Lama or the Pope would approve of. I saw hate there, and anger, and defiance, and frustration. And at that moment I wished she'd slapped me back, even harder, maybe several times, but she didn't. Her cheek turned the color of a ripe tomato, her face contracted itself into a wrinkled ball, and tears began pouring out of her squeezed-shut eyes.

We were in the living room when it happened, it's a small room, maybe a little bigger than a room at the Motel 6. And through the archway is the dining room, and beyond that the kitchen with brown linoleum on the floor that's supposed to look like Mexican tile, and down the hall are the two bedrooms and the bathroom. That's the whole house, where I brought her up, it's not big but it's clean and everything works. We were standing in the middle of the living room and behind her, on the 32-inch Sony, I could see Oprah waving her arms and she had a look on her face like she smelled something bad, and she was saying "How could you do that? How could you slap your sweet daughter?" Several million people were watching, and they all knew it was me she was talking to.

"Well, Oprah, it's like this," I said. "I've tried to do the right thing by her."

A woman in the audience groaned, one of those "I don't believe this guy" groans, shaking her head, her face as severe as a nun. I said to her, "Look, lady, you know nothing about it. My Mary walked out on me when Darlene was only five, and I raised her the best I could, and now for my trouble I get a daughter who's screwing every Tom, Dick and Harry, what do I know, maybe she's the town pump for Christ sake."

And the audience woman just shook her head slowly and said "Tsk, tsk, tsk." I could have killed her.

I guess this was the big moment my life had been leading up to, it was the American dream all right, the American dream come true. When I became an adult I got married and got a job like you're supposed to, and put a roof over our heads and lugged home the bacon. And we brought a baby into the world, a beautiful little girl. And then, just like the soaps Mary used to watch, she ups and leaves me, she needs her space she tells me, needs to discover herself, and I keep living the dream on my own, with baby Darlene. And now here we were, my baby daughter all grown up and screwing around (and yours is too, don't forget that), and me slapping her, and Oprah embarrassing me in front of millions, and a nun woman going "tsk, tsk, tsk." That's what it had come to.

"I'm sorry," I said finally, my anger spent. "Sweetie, I am so sorry."

"Fuck you," she said, her face still crumpled and red and wet. "Fuck you, fuck you, fuck you."

"Nobody deserves what I just did," I said. "Nobody deserves to be slapped like that."

"Nobody," she said.

"Nobody," said Oprah.

"Nobody," said the lady with the nun face.

"Nobody, nobody, nobody," chanted the audience.

Later that night Darlene had gone off to who knows where, and I sat in front of the 32-incher in my favorite chair, a burgundy velour La-Z-Boy recliner that's mellowed to fit my body just right. And on the TV was a news story about the war in Iraq, and some kids who had been killed by a bomb in a Baghdad marketplace, and to see their limp little bodies made me cry. I thought of Darlene, when she was just five or six, sweet and innocent, and it just made me cry, everything I did not understand, there in my La-Z-Boy chair, living my American dream.

The Fall

The penalty for stumbling
blind your chosen path
is to fall much further
and faster than you would think
possible for men
gifted with wings stolen
from angels.

Entirely Without Regret

Wanda plunged through the wet sheets dangling on the clothesline, bare feet slipping and sliding on the bathroom floor. I held my breath. Cracked skull. Blood sipping through her small, pink mouth. Blood dropping out of her pointy nose. Eyes staring coldly at the flickering neon lights above.

Damn these hard tiles. They can kill a person. Wanda skidded to a halt, turned, and peered through the polka-dotted pillowcases. Thank God. No waiting in line at the overcrowded emergency room today. For a moment I thought I had her. Her little lips were twitching, deciding on whether to let out a high-pitched wail or start laughing. "Wanda, for the last time. Here." I tried sounding cheerful, holding out her dirty red rubber boots. Living with a two-and-a-half-year-old is like living with a mad, abusive drunk. With their giddy laughter, they make your life paradise one moment, only to turn it into hell the next with their aggressive Kim Jong-style outbursts. Wanda ducked away behind the dots. "Do you want to get into your boots yourself, or do you want me to do it?" I asked, putting all my hopes on the good, old "two-choices" method. Wanda shook her head, those brown tangled curls bobbing up and down, lips pressed together in a thin, straight line. She crossed her chubby arms over her chest and frowned.

"No," she stated simply.

"Wanda. We need to go. Mommy is in a hurry." If I were to walk toward her decidedly, she would bolt again; I knew that much. So I remained where I was, the clothesline between us like a net in some game. "Wanda will stay home today," she said then, matter-of-factly, bending over, starting to peel off her pink pantaloons. The very same pantaloons it had taken me half an hour to put on. The very same pantaloons that had kicked me in my face while that insane eel wiggled out of my grasp, wailing *No! Nooooooooo!* so loud, I thought my eardrums would burst.

"Don't take off your pants! Honey! *Please!*"

Like she cared. She threw them over her head and grinned like a gangster after a killing shot. An EWR-smile. Entirely Without Regret.

I wanted to cry. I wanted to hide in a cupboard, nursing my wounded feelings. *I gave up my whole life for you and you kick me in the face?* I hated this whiny voice in my head, but it had become a constant companion lately. God, I wished I were one of those mothers who could make their kids do anything with a friendly command and a joke. Instead I had to bite my tongue not to say what I was really thinking.

If you don't put on your boots, I will not cook for you or change your stinky diaper ever again.

If you don't put on your boots, I won't ever play with you again, because playing with you is boring and I only do it because I have to.

If you don't put on your boots, I will smack your little behind until you learn how to behave the way I had to, you spoiled little shit.

Wanda took off her cardigan too, while she was at it. I sighed, squatting down. Some leader, not being able to grab a toddler and be on my way. Doctor Lin would have to wait another three months. Mommy would have to pay 140 pounds for nothing. The stupid test that would decide if I could have another baby could go where the sun doesn't shine.

Fuck it.

Wanda was not the only one who could put up a fight. I pulled off my T-shirt. A musky, unpleasant odor rose from my armpits. I didn't even recognize my own smell anymore.

Fuck it.

I sat down and pulled off my socks and jeans. Wanda stared at me suspiciously. I grabbed a sock and dressed my ear with it. And there was sock number two. I pulled it over the other ear. "OK. I am off," I said calmly, scrambling up without as much as a blink in her direction, ears flopping. I hummed a tune while dropping my keys into my bag and drinking the last slosh of cold coffee. I heard Wanda sneaking out of the bathroom then. I could feel her standing behind me, holding on

114

to the doorframe. "I want an ice cream," she tried uncertainly. "Why don't you go buy one?" I sailed past the stunned little girl and opened the front door. "I have an appointment." Instantly, a gush of cold rain hit my naked legs. "Bye, sweetie," I sang, taking a step outside. The wet stone was slippery under my bare feet. Spitting drops plastered my hair to my head. Mr. Neds hurried past then, red-faced and sweaty, glancing up from under his umbrella.

"Good morning, Gabriella!" The man stopped. He blinked a few times, stared at my breasts, at the socks dangling from my ears, then turned to look at the neat row of semi-detached houses, as if wondering if he was in quite the right place. He pushed his spectacles up his sweaty nose, shifted his huge body, and hurried away without another word. I realized I was grinning, wide. It was a long time since I had enjoyed myself this much.

"Not go without shoes, Mommy!" Wanda demanded loudly. She came toward me, carrying a pair of old boots and that Kim Jong-frown of hers.

"Oh," I said, "I am just gonna go like this."

"Mommy put on your *boots*!" she demanded strictly.

I crossed my arms over my chest.

"Do as I say!" Wanda threatened.

Deep down beneath, something grumbled and lurched. There was no stopping it. It was charging like a wild animal. *Do as I say. As I say. Do as I. Say.* The words echoed infinitely in my mind, bouncing back and forth like in a house of mirrors of sound. *Do as I say.* The voice was my mother's, raw and dry. I felt sick. Her cold, blue eyes burrowed into mine. It was like looking into an abyss of hate.

That's when I slipped. Soaking wet, I fell flat on my back. A shrill spasm shot through my ribcage, up and down the spine, foot to skull. Tears streamed down my cheeks. A cold wind tugged at my hair. Shame flooded my head as the prim houses came back into focus.

A small, warm hand on my forehead, full of tenderness and compassion. Wanda bent down on all fours and angled her sweet face so she could look at me, take me all in. In silence she stroked my head.

115

The love of this two-and-a-half-year-old entered me slowly, like a cruise ship coming toward a harbor. How I wanted it. How I wanted the softness and the kindness. And how it scared me. At once I wanted to sit up and shield myself. Shield myself by talking, by complaining about the pain, by running away to who knows where. Anything but feeling this thing, this choice that now stood before me. At this moment, laying almost naked on a wet staircase in a London suburb, looking into the warm gaze of my child, I realized I had never felt really loved before. I realized I had never dared to. I had never dared to let love in, had never let the ship of love take anchor inside me. I could either close up now or force myself to have the courage to feel all this vulnerability and longing. But I was not really in a position to run. So I opened up. Just a little. Just for that moment.

All shame disappeared and instead I was overwhelmed with shyness. "I am stupid," I tried meekly. Wanda shook her head, her hand still on my face. "You are not stupid, Mum, sometimes one just doesn't want to wear boots."

I had to smile. It felt so good lying there, simply not wanting to wear boots, letting the rain soak both of us. I was tired, so tired of having to be perfect, of having to do everything perfectly. "I want cookies," I declared.

"Me too!" came the enthusiastic response next to me.

Wanda held my hand as we limped down the corridor at the emergency room. "Look, mommy!" she cried, poking at my hand. "We are not the only ones who don't want to wear boots today."

Grief Plan

Don't write poems about your sadness,
sensible people will head for the exits,
except the wrong ones, some of them,
who see opportunity in sobbing.

Don't cry on every shoulder you come upon.
You don't have the tears for so much irrigation
and you may get stuck with dry cleaning bills.

Instead make a schedule for weeping and keep to it.
Every ten minutes should do.
Over the years try stretching this out
to eleven or thirteen.

Then find a good heart, a person who knows you,
someone whose heart has been broken themselves.
I recommend a loving sister.
Feel them pat you on the back and say
I know. I know. I know.

How to Get Rid of a Ghost
(and Other Lessons from Camp Pispogutt)

It's lucky that Pispogutt rhymes with lots of things. I have the campers close their eyes and make up poems while I hide Russian nesting dolls around the perimeter of the nature cabin. There's a red cardinal that I bought on clearance at a craft store that counts as extra points for whoever finds it first. The game isn't over until every nesting doll has been rescued from makeshift shelters of moss and slippery elm bark. Sometimes I throw other wild cards into the treasure hunt. Indian pipes. Forget-me-nots. Hemlock sprigs. This is my fall back exercise for when I'm too hung over to think up anything original. Which is nearly every day.

I try not to talk to my ghost in front of other people. This morning I don't even want to look at her. She kept me up nearly all night with the clickety-clack of her silver knitting needles. I know she's pissed about being ignored, because when I take the children out to the fire circle to practice building fires she keeps blowing out the tiny flames. The campers get so discouraged that I leave them alone long enough to sneak inside the cabin for a quick slug of vodka.

"You've got a drinking problem," my ghost says, materializing in the doorway. The air between us turns frosty. "There's little kids playing with fire unchaperoned out there."

"You're my drinking problem." I tell her. I've dribbled a little down my shirt, which bears the proud Camp Pispogutt logo in a bright, hopeful canary yellow. Just beneath it is a rising sun.

She laughs. Wind chimes tinkling in the breeze. "Tell it to a therapist," she says. "Or better yet, explain it to your boss."

My boss is a large, formerly-Jewish, recently-converted Zen Buddhist called Bear. He has a five year plan to turn Camp Pispogutt into a mindfulness meditation retreat for families. I know this because he showed me his dream manifestation board during my initial interview. It features a collage that includes pictures of the rustic six-acre camp, magazine cut-outs from different five-star resorts, and pasted in snippets of Buddhist prayer and meditation.

At our camp training, he had Doshinji monks come down from the Catskills and stay a weekend with us so we could all learn how to be attuned to our surroundings. Most of them had names like Brother Sun and Sister Smile. They took us on a lot of slow walks through the forest.

"Imagine your feet are kissing the earth with each step," Brother Sun would say.

I staggered along, drunk as a lord, wondering why the monks couldn't see my ghost. On the last day of their visit I broke down on a yoga mat to Brother Sun.

I guess confessing to monks is something like confessing to priests. Brother Sun never said anything to Bear about our discussion. I begged for help, but he was a kind wall of brown-robed detachment.

"You need to clear your mind of impurities," he said, solemn faced and serious. "There is energy. There is the spirit. We create personal versions of this."

It was the first and only time I mentioned my ghost to another person.

Of course, *she* heard the whole thing. She was furious. She didn't speak to me for days afterwards. Silent treatment from a ghost doesn't sound bad, but it is. It's nerve-wracking. Quiet haunting is the most unpredictable.

~~~

"Go ahead, Regan, try it," she says now. "Spill the beans and see who believes you." She's still laughing. She pulls herself up into the tall branches of a maple tree and twirls around. I go back outside just in time. One of the younger kids has figured out how to get a pile of leaves to smolder with a magnifying glass and a shard of sunlight.

My ghost especially loves the nature cabin. It's full of the husks of dead things. Butterflies, beetles, bird nests, old skulls and vertebrae of all sorts of animals from mice, to muskrats, to giant elk. It's a bone yard of the living, breathing forest outside. I teach the campers about our surroundings by tracing outward from what's left behind. We never talk about it, but I think she is drawn to the bones because hers were never found.

On good days my ghost sits on the splintery counters following along with the lessons with some interest. On the bad days, like today, she torments me and plays pranks on the campers. It leaves me feeling dismal and down.

Even later that afternoon when I've got a pretty strong buzz and a group of campers spots a nest with perfect sky-blue robin's eggs in it, I still have to pretend to be thrilled. I hardly notice the colors or the teacup china quality to the eggs. Instead I'm glaring at my ghost who is tying two campers' shoelaces together.

In life we weren't like this. In life we were friends.

~~~

Ghosts aside, I'm not a very good employee. In between groups of children I swig heartily from a water bottle full of vodka in my backpack, smoke cigarettes behind my cabin, and pop Xanax and breath mints like candy. I give myself regular rubdowns with insect repellent and hand sanitizer to cover the scent. Perfume would be too suspicious around here. I do my best not to sweat. Not an easy task outdoors in the summer. I try to come up with low energy, nature-oriented tasks for the campers. We harvest a lot of butterfly eggs. Once we've ravaged the milkweed supply on one side of the tennis courts, we move on to catching newts and salamanders.

"Finally," she says, hanging upside down from a tree branch as we turn over logs and splash through streams. "I am so sick of watching you scrape eggs with plastic spoons. At least these things move."

Her blond hair dangles down in baby fine wisps that snake out to taste the spicy forest air. I want to tell her she doesn't have to hang

120

around and watch all the time. But I can't yell at her in front of the campers.

"Please," I hiss. "Please go away."

I turn my attention to a little girl who's balanced on a rotten log. There are living things that need my help right now.

I blame a lot on her. Things happen. Things that seem like omens, or something worse. Someone puts tadpoles in the Kool-aid. I find a hognose snake in the cabin, mistake it for a copperhead, and sever its head with a shovel in front of some campers before realizing my error. Juniper, the much beloved, injured flying squirrel we're taking care of, gives birth and eats her own kits. I find the nest full of blood and tiny, transparent limbs in the morning. Birds fly into the screened windows, batting their beaks against the wire mesh, poking holes for swarms of mosquitoes to fly in. I take the campers wading through a pond to catch bullfrogs and we all end up covered in leeches that crawl quickly up under our pants and above our knees. This results in a Bacchalian display of frenzied nudity in the forest.

I can't prove she's behind it, but I think she is. She rolls on the banks laughing as I pull slimy parasites from pale, white, quivering adolescent thighs.

One day there is a thunderstorm so fierce that we all have to crowd inside the small, rickety cabin. In the pitching shadows and rumbling darkness of the storm it feels like we're in a ship. My ghost crawls around the ceiling knocking mice nests from the rafters onto our heads. The kids scream. They panic. They jostle terrariums full of newts and spiders. I have to radio down to the main office for extra counselor backup. She looks pleased at my inability to handle the situation.

"You're an asshole," I say. We glare at each other. In life we weren't like this. In life we were friends.

Bear sends up one of the lifeguards who takes in the scene with some horror. I have the five and six year olds this afternoon. Stuck in the nature cabin with me and a ghost during a thunderstorm they're a small herd of stampeding cattle. They squash newts and trample bird bones. I can't blame them. She's breathing on the backs of their necks. The whites of their eyes roll around with terror.

"Christ, Regan," the lifeguard says, even though we aren't supposed to curse on camp property. His name is Bay and he's worked here for a few summers now. A lot of the staff began as former counselors. They're a tight click. No room for a girl and her ghost.

"It's like the Little Shop of Horrors in here. Let's just take them down to the mess hall and wait out the worst of it."

The mess hall is through a patch of forest, across the tennis courts, and down a large hill. It has a tin roof. It's not the safest place to shelter a thunderstorm, but I don't argue with him. It's a giant, open air pavilion with plenty of benches and no specimen jars or poisonous animals. We do a head count, pair the kids up, and Bay takes the front while I hold up the rear of the line. My ghost trails through the rain after us, laughing at the thunder and holding her palms up towards the sky. I'm not surprised to see her behind me. She follows me everywhere.

In life *she* wasn't like this. Dying has given her some kind of dark edge that makes her unpredictable and terribly codependent. Her mood swings are mercurial. I can't trust them. I can't trust her. This is mostly because of the nets she makes at night when she thinks I am sleeping. I'm pretty sure she is planning on suffocating me.

~~~

"You've got circles under your eyes," Bay says.

The kids have calmed down now. A few of the smaller ones who are scared of thunder huddle against us, but for the most part it's turned into an adventure for them. Bay is tall and strong and brings an aura of lifeguard safety wherever he goes. The campers run around the picnic tables playing tag.

"Really, you look like shit," he says, ear-muffing the little boy beside him. "Maybe you should move back into the cabins. And definitely get checked out by the nurse."

We're sitting on the top of a picnic table. The spray of cold rain bounces off the grass and mists over us. She's dancing out there.

122

Spinning in circles, her thin dress stuck to her body. Delighting in the heavy thunder cracks and white flashes that zigzag over the trees. There's nothing a nurse can do for me.

"I'm fine," I say. "I like sleeping out in the open. Those cabins make me claustrophobic."

All of the other specialists and instructors share cabins. The counselors sleep with the campers. I stay in my own tent at the edge of Beaver Pond, even though I don't like beavers. It's isolated from the rest of the camp and hidden from view by Big Poppa, a giant rocky precipice that is off limits to the campers. Bear agreed to this because I told him it was part of my solitary journey to attain spiritual enlightenment. Really, I need a few hours where I can stop pretending. Pretending my dead friend isn't following my every move. Pretending I don't need a lot of liquor to make it manageable. Pretending I'm not falling apart.

In the evenings, after camp lessons are over, Bay and the others sit out by the lake and socialize and tell each other stories about their days. They have nicknames for everyone. The kids. The directors. I don't know what they are.

"Do I have a nickname?" I ask.

He makes a face. "A nickname? No but you should."

"Dances with Salamanders," I say.

"Swims with Muskrats."

"Flies with Bats."

"Travels with Ghost."

She's beside me suddenly, her dress transparent on her skin. Raindrops hanging off her eyelashes. "Say it," she urges, her lips curved into a half moon that really isn't a smile at all. Just a half moon. "Say Travels with Ghost."

She leans across me and holds her face so close to Bay's that their noses almost touch. "That's why she doesn't sleep in the cabins. Because she has me."

If Bay could see her he would be awestruck. When she was alive she was stunning. As a ghost she is magnificent. All glowing and

123

golden and long-limbed. Ethereal. At least that's the way she looks when she knows I am watching her. Sometimes at night I see her drawn up in the corners of my tent like a crouching spider. She's taken to knitting as soon as I get in my sleeping bag. I usually pull up the drawstrings around my head and count fireflies blinking on the thin shell of the tent outside. Bullfrogs chorus around the lake. Water laps at the rocky shore. It still takes me at least a half a pint of whiskey before I can fall asleep to the clicking rhythm of her gleaming ghost needles.

Even though he doesn't see or hear her, Bay shivers and rubs at the gooseflesh spreading across his arms. "I think you're becoming feral," he says. "You're spending too much time with children and wild animals."

"She's a drunk," my ghost informs him.

"You should try being around a group of your peers." He smiles. "It really doesn't hurt."

"Says Mr. Lifeguard," she says with a sigh. "Do you want me to tell you how many of the counselors he's slept with? You're killing me, Regan. You used to be smart and fun."

She launches herself away from us and back into the grass doing cartwheels and backhand springs.

"I'm fun," I tell Bay, conversationally. "Last week I made up a song about a butterfly named Omoscis who drinks nectar with his proboscis. The campers loved it."

~~~

By the third week of camp, I'm getting awfully paranoid. I've become convinced she can hear my thoughts. Most of them revolve around her and how to make her go away. I'm also worried that the old man who works at the liquor store in the nearby town, where Bear sends me to get supplies, is going to squeal about how much vodka I buy every week. These hill towns are small. Every time I get radioed to come down to the main office, I'm sure someone will notice that I'm drunk. Or question my liquor store purchases.

I dispose of the evidence by burning cigarette butts and plastic liquor bottles. I transfer most of my stash into water bottles before I return to camp. I am bug-sprayed and sanitized to the point that my flesh should be peeling off.

"You're a regular crime scene," my ghost says.

I also swim a lot. I like Bay and I like the smell of lake water drying on my skin. There are lots of salamanders down by the lifeguard station so I have a hardy stock of them in rows of aquariums in the nature cabin. Some have laid eggs. We observe their different life cycles: me, my campers, and my ghost.

"They're the only animal in the world that goes from aquatic to terrestrial and back to aquatic again. That means that they have gills first, and then grow lungs and feet. They live on land for up to eight years, traveling far and wide, before switching back to gills, shrinking their legs, and returning into the water as salamanders. Some newts even do this several times."

I wow them appropriately by sticking my hand in a terrarium and pulling out a squirming, juvenile red-eft newt, neon-orange with soft, poisonous skin. The kind that are abundant in this early, wet part of summer. The kids ooh and ahh and my ghost entertains herself by keeping the feathers that are tied to the rafters spinning overhead. She's already heard this spiel half a dozen times today. She's seen a couple handfuls of newts.

We move on to the salamanders. I pull one out of the tank and it flops around in my hands. There is something about their eyes. They look blind in their aquatic stage. They creep the kids out a little and I understand why. It's hard to trust something that changes so completely that it becomes an entirely different animal. They gaze at the salamander tanks with interest, but no one ever wants to hold them.

"So how do they do it?" my ghost asks after the kids have gone.

I've stoked the firepit outside the cabin and I'm grilling a burger. I don't eat a lot these days. My curves are trimmed away, leaving hollows in my cheeks and making caverns of my clavicles.

125

"Do what?" I take another gulp of my vodka water bottle and squint at her through the smoke. She doesn't disappear. Instead she lights the tips of her fingers on fire and blows them out carefully. My stomach lurches. I abandon the burger.

"How do they change back and forth like that? From newt to salamander."

"Magic," I tell her. I don't know how they do it. I'm a pretty crap nature specialist even without the alcoholism. Bear didn't hire me for my qualifications. He hired me because I told him about the accident. After she died I knew I didn't want to waste anymore of my life. I quit my bartending job to find something meaningful and fulfilling. I wanted to influence and change lives. I wanted to work at Camp Pispogutt.

"I don't invest in things, I invest in people," he'd said after my speech, clasping me in a hug that explained his name. "There's a reason you found me. Welcome aboard, Regan."

That was the night my ghost showed up. She was sitting cross-legged in the middle of my bedroom when I got home, examining a stack of her own records that her parents had insisted I keep. I had packed her clothes away in giant lawn and leaf bags to bring to a donation center. They were unpacked and strewn around my room in a violent explosion of patterns and colors. It was exactly three weeks after she'd died. It was the first step I'd taken away from her.

~~~

On my day off, I drive to the closest library that has wifi. The main office at camp has a computer, but I don't want anyone to see what I'm researching.

"Where are we going?" she asks? Her hair is a puff of silk out the open window. Her profile is perfect. She chain smokes along with me, blowing smoke rings into the shapes of animals that skate off into the sky. Her knitting bag is on the passenger-side floor beneath her feet. I turn up the music and drive fast along the country roads.

There's no easy way to do this.

At the library, I browse through the books for a while. It's a small town library. I don't expect to find anything I'm looking for, but I take a few manuals about regional edible plants and wild animals.

"You've already researched that stuff," she comments. She wanders off to look in the art section. In life she loved to paint. It must not have stuck, because she's back in a flash, looking over my shoulder at the computer screen as I type HOW TO GET RID OF A GHOST. The good thing about becoming a full blown alcoholic is that I have a water bottle in my purse at the ready. I can get drunk anywhere. The warmth that settles over my insides as I read doesn't stop me from noticing that she's crying, but it makes me feel a little less.

The Universal Psychic Guild is no help at all. What I'm dealing with is beyond a poltergeist. It's a full blown incarnation of my best friend. Most of what I find online is fairly unhelpful. I read the signs of supernatural interference: hearing voices, objects appearing or disappearing, electronics turning on and off by themselves, hallucinations, feelings of being watched, animals acting strangely, a sudden urge to overeat, drink, smoke, or do drugs, and nightmares. All understatements. But then, I never doubted I was haunted anyways.

My ghost reads the next steps out loud as I scan them:

1) Identify the energy. Higher level guides are not abusive or negative. If your ghost is a loved one who died, realize that it's better for both of you if they go to the Light.

2) Sometimes ghosts don't realize they're dead or being bothersome. Therefore, firmly yet calmly explain out loud that he or she is dead, and it's time to move on to the Light (point upwards). Make sure you are sober and centered during this process or you'll open yourself up to the risk of possession.

3) If the energy does not want to leave, call in God, guides of the Light, and for tougher cases, archangels Michael and Sandalphon for assistance in guiding the lost soul(s) to the Light.

~~~

We leave the library in silence. Inside the car I say, "Listen, it's not because I don't want you to be here."

127

She doesn't answer me. Her face is tear-streaked and looks like thunder. I want to feel sorry for her, but I know what she wants. She wants my body. She wants my bones.

"It's not right," I say. I'm dressed in her clothes. Waify, fluttery garments that she snuck into the suitcase I took to camp. She replaced all of my things with her own. When I look in the mirror I hardly see myself anymore.

"You aren't supposed to be here."

"You're so selfish, Regan," she says. Her eyes are solid black. "You're half the reason I'm here you know. The least you can do is share your life with me. And you won't even do that."

Each word is a punch to the gut. I take my time going back to camp. We drive through the mountains taking in the bright green of new leaves and swirling mist tendrils that soften the forest into someplace magical. I do it for her. She's not staying here.

"And if you try any of that new-agey, sage-burning, walking to the light bullshit with me then I really will possess you," she threatens, slumping down in her seat.

When I'd checked my email at the library there were several messages from her parents. She'd read them over my shoulder with childish satisfaction. Each one was a heartbreaking avowal of a parent's grief for their dead child. It's this type of thing that makes me feel like my ghost isn't the girl that I knew. In life that would never make her happy.

Since it's my day off, I drink whiskey the whole way back. The sun becomes a slanted shimmering thing. I sing along to the radio with soulful abandon. I buy a bucket of red paint and some brushes. I don't slow down when I get to the long dirt road that leads through Camp Pispogutt property. Instead I bounce off potholes and send shimmering sprays off micah flecked dust up behind me.

"I feel fine," I tell her. "I'm great."

She taps her fingers on the console. "I will never forgive you," she says.

I shake a Xanax into my hand, and take another drink.

128

~~~

By the time we get back to camp, I feel as if I am swimming. The afternoon is a drop of amber. Everything has that slightly surreal quality, as if time has turned thick and slowed down. It's why I like being drunk on whiskey. I feel burnt and liquid at the same time. I don't waste any time. I carry the bucket of red paint through the forest and paint two coats on the door of the nature cabin. Red repels ghosts. At least I hope it does.

Juniper, the filicidal flying squirrel, watches me from her bird cage. I haul the cage outside and open the hinged slider, and then go back inside so she can escape on her own terms. The red-eft newts have been captive for over a month now. I carry the terrariums out next to the empty cage and dump them out, watching their neon skins disappear into the mossy earth. Then the salamanders. The aquariums are too heavy to lift, but I scoop them up with a net and transfer them to the campfire water bucket.

"What are you doing?" my ghost demands as I return to our campsite and lower the bucket into Beaver Pond. The salamanders swim away like gun shots under water.

~~~

I change into the bikini that I wasn't supposed to bring to camp. The one my ghost used to replace the standard navy one-piece I bought to accommodate Pispogutt regulations. The waterfront dock floats. Water spiders scurry up through the cracks beneath my feet as I walk down to the deepest part of the swimming area.

Bay waves from the shore where he's teaching the Minnow age swimmers how to tread water. A few of the campers shout my name. I'm a surprising favorite with the kids. Several have adopted my/ghost's style of wearing silk scarves as bandanas, and short skirts with galoshes. The older girls braid feathers and flowers into their hair. I've taught them how to make scotch tape nature bracelets, by ringing their wrists with inside-out tape and pressing leaves, ferns, acorn caps, flower petals, and berries to the sticky side in order to fashion personalized forest accessories.

129

I dive into the lake and swim. I breaststroke until I'm out of breath and crampy and Bay is signaling for me to start swimming back to shore.

"Your schoolgirl crush is pathetic," she says. She floats on her back wearing oversized sunglasses. "Do you really think he would like you if he knew the things I do about you?"

I swim back towards the shore underwater. I can't hear her. I can't see her. It's blessed silence. Just me and the salamanders. So there are places she can't get at me. I climb back up onto the dock.

"You're quite the swimmer," says Bay.

Afternoon lessons with the campers are over. The other lifeguards are closing up the swimming area. I help Bay pick up discarded life jackets and carry them into the boathouse. I'm still drunk, but the water must have washed the smell of booze away because he doesn't seem to notice.

"Do you have any snorkels?" I ask. "And a mask maybe?"

"Sure," he says. He has a white strip of suntan lotion on his nose. His arms are tanned and muscled. He's vigorously alive. "But you can't see too much in the lake. It's pretty cloudy."

I don't care. I'm imagining hours of uninterrupted silence underwater. He digs out a pair of each and hands them to me.

"Just don't go swimming alone," he says. "Bear would kill me. Buddy system. Even for the adults. Come get me if you want to swim."

I nod. My mood's improved a hundred percent.

"Wow," says Bay. "You're smiling."

"Like an idiot," my ghost says.

He smiles back. "What are you doing with the rest of your day off?"

~~~

We have sex in the boat room. Then in the water. The campers and counselors are at dinner so we have the lakefront to ourselves. I try out my new swimming gear and make a mental note to myself to write an online post next time I go to the library. Ghosts can't bother you when

130

you're snorkeling underwater. And you don't notice them so much when you're having sex with a good looking lifeguard.

"You should come down to the bonfire," he says. It's a weekly camp event that includes all of the campers, instructors, and staff. I've never participated before. I know Bear likes to play the bongo drums and has replaced traditional Pispogutt camp songs with some of the ditties that the Doshinji monks taught us during training. I have a blurry recollection of them. Songs to fall asleep to.

"Why not," I say.

"What?" my ghost asks.

"Great," says Bay. "I'll make us some sandwiches. You should put dry clothes on. It's getting cold."

"You have to be kidding me!" shouts my ghost. "What are you doing, Regan? First this idiot and now campfire songs with a bunch of brainwashed morons? If you think this is going to cure you, you are so wrong."

I ignore her and strip out of my wet bathing suit, hanging it on a branch to dry. I pull on one of her lacy shirts, jeans that hang on my hip bones now, and a striped hoodie that has thumbholes poked in the cuffs. The whiskey's done a number on my stomach so I switch to vodka, smoke a cigarette, and then perfume myself with bug spray and tea tree oil. I pop a mint in my mouth. She moves above me in the tree tops, angrily shaking the leaves.

Bay meets me by Big Poppa and we walk up to the bonfire spot together. There's a big moon tonight and the stars are bright and low hanging. Fireflies blink on the path around us. The air is spicy and clean. We eat our cheese sandwiches in silence. I wouldn't say I feel happy exactly. My ghost is still there. She makes rude comments the whole time. Still, it's the farthest I've felt from alone in a while.

"Do they tell ghost stories at the bonfire?" I ask.

Bay shakes his head. "Bear doesn't like that. As of this year there are no ghosts at Camp Pispogutt."

My ghost snorts.

"Did there used to be?" I ask.

131

Bay gives me a fiendish smile. "The Goatman. He lived in that abandoned shack down past the nature cabin. Where we keep the tennis nets."

I know exactly where he's talking about

"There's no Goatman," my ghost says, thoroughly annoyed.

"What was his story?" I ask.

Bay shrugs. "The usual. Ate little kids. Bad campers. Played pranks. The subject of campfire stories. I think he was half goat, but I don't remember why."

"Why would a ghost eat a kid?" she asks.

"How did Bear get rid of him?"

Bay gives me a funny look. "Because he never existed, Regan. You are strange sometimes. Bear just outlawed telling ghost stories. They aren't very Zen, you know?"

My ghost takes offense at this, but we've reached the bonfire. I sit beside Bay. Bear is indeed playing a pair of bongos. The camp music teacher has a guitar and someone else is playing a triangle. It's amazing that I've been here half the summer and I hardly know anyone aside from the campers.

I vaguely remember the song they're singing from orientation. The lyrics consist mostly of the words *breathe in, breathe out.* I can't quite bring myself to sing along. Behind me my ghost has made herself comfortable. I tip my head slightly to one side and hear the click-click-click of her knitting needles. She works in tempo with the music.

I watch the firelight lick at the faces around me. The words blur. The sounds change. My eyes become heavy-lidded and sleepy.

"I feel funny," I tell Bay, but he doesn't seem to hear me.

I tug at his sleeve but he remains impassive.

All of the sudden, my stomach is churning violently. I get to my feet, stagger over to the bushes, and begin to projectile vomit. My lips are slimy and taste like lake. Beneath me are squirming masses of slick-bellied shining salamanders.

132

Everything tilts. The music is pounding at my head. I can't see my ghost. I can't find Bay. I can't even make out the faces of the people sitting around the fire. Everything is strange and foreign.

I lunge down the hill towards the bathrooms. I'm going to be sick again. I have the sudden fear that I'll throw up newts this time. Or the disembodied parts of newborn squirrels.

"Hey," says my ghost. She's come after me. "It's okay, Regan, I'm here."

I open my mouth to speak and begin vomiting again. I close my eyes so I can't see what it is. I wipe something wet from my chin.

"Come on." She's helping me. We're walking away from the music. Away from the bathrooms and back down towards our campsite. I stop to throw up again on Big Poppa. This time I look. *Leeches*. I fall backwards and scramble away, coughing the last few up in long, stretchy pieces.

"You're just hallucinating, Regan," she says, trying to still my panic. She looks beautiful in the moonlight. I can't be hallucinating. There's blood all over my mouth.

She hands me my vodka and I gargle with it. I rinse my face and chin. I gulp it down greedily hoping it will kill anything that's still inside. After a long while my stomach finally settles. I want to go inside the tent and crawl into my sleeping bag but I can't move. I'm too exhausted.

My ghost is knitting. I lay in the grass and she perches on a rock above me. Stars spin as her knitting needles flash and gleam and click. Something settles over me like a blanket. Soft strands. Silken threads. They wave across my cheek like ripples of water. Then they become stronger. Weedier. Full of all kinds of things. Dappled sunlight, green vines, fireflies, dead butterflies, and bluebird feathers. It's hard to breathe. I feel around for my snorkel.

I *am* underwater.

I lay flat on my belly at the bottom of the lake. Cool mud. Feathery water ferns. I see the top part of a Russian nesting doll half-buried in the glittering silt. I have always loved the way the surface looks from

133

underneath. It fractures the moonlight and turns fireflies into glowing embers. I try to push the weeds away to see them better. From down here they look like the remains of leftover campfires.

With Miniature House

Not because she wanted to abandon this domesticity
or even because
she crafted snapped twigs into tiny fuses. Not because
she had been
hiding them under her mattress for months: these
minute peelings of bark
and sorrow. Or how many days smoke could be seen
through the keyhole.

First she was paper, once wood. Then wood, once
tree. The tree, hewn
box which holds her. She might have been anything.
Like tinder, fuel, kindling.
Or one timbered beam: sudden sky, heavenly
opening. She was that, or she
was the timbrel of the entire house, collapsing.

It could have been the curtains crafted from cut
snow: lace-paper flakes the color
of curdled cream. In the kitchen, a table strewn with
stationery, pen. It could have
been that she's written an argument for longevity,
tissue-thin. Perfume your head.
Bake diminutive cakes. Put on your death-dress, and
go on living.

Or that she fed the fire. And that the fire fed on itself.
Windows concave:

an inhale. Then convex. One long breath-puff, and
breaks. Each room, a little
container: flint, steel, small spark. This bonfire in
darkness and just enough
to torch the quarreling trees and ruined light.

The Cat Face

All roads lead to Rome, sputtered Brucie, pounding his stick on the fence.

But I'm not interested in Rome, answered Earl. I'm just interested in getting home.

The brothers had a long walk before them; at least two hours. Earl walked with his cold hands thrust into his pockets. Brucie swung the stick ahead.

Cold today, muttered Earl.

Yes. Cold—you know if we walked the tracks we'd get there faster.

The tracks—

Yes. Between Ryder's lane and Washington Avenue. We cut across. It'll save fifteen minutes. We won't have to go all the way around.

Okay.

They reached the railroad crossing and cut over down the tracks. The ties were rotted and the rails were crooked. The line had not been used for years. They walked. It's when Brucie saw it laying between the tracks.

Look, said Brucie—a little skull.

He poked the skull with his stick. It rolled across.

No no no said Earl—don't break it—

He picked it up.

Look at those teeth, he said.

What kind of skull is it—

My guess is it's a cat's skull—look there's a little hair still on it. And a little flesh.

Yes, said Brucie, fingering it—it looks that way.

Oh well, said Earl—and he slipped it in his coat pocket. They walked along, Brucie tapping his stick on the rail. Scrub brush passed them on other side, and sandy dunes.

This is a Godforsaken place, said Brucie.

No—not really, said Earl, as he felt the cat skull round and hard in his pocket.

The grey sky lowered above them and there were no shadows—just the darkness nestling in the low brown brush passing them by.

Earl gripped the skull. The hand in his other pocket was empty. He scratched at his palm with his fingertips. His nails were long. Earl's fingers found their way into the empty eye sockets of the skull. It was a face—a little face. He rubbed the teeth. He stumbled over a tie but did not fall. Brucie said, Be careful Earl. You almost fell down.

No I didn't.

Looked like you did to me.

He pressed the eye sockets.

No I didn't.

He clasped his hand over the cat face. He felt the nose hole, the teeth. He thought of the live cat they had at the house—the grey striped tabby. This could be its face. He ran his hand over the furry side of the cat—the cat rose and slunk away and left the room. He squeezed the cat face in his pocket. He spoke to Brucie.

What do you think Mom will make for dinner tonight?

Who's to tell? said Brucie, tapping the rail sliding by.

Earl put one finger in the eye of the cat face and left the other finger touching the tip of a tooth and thought of the cat's food down in the olive dish on the floor in the dining room. The food was dry and brown. What had the cat face eaten—mice, probably. He pressed a finger to the front teeth of the cat face. It was in the darkness within the warmth of his hand. What food had passed those teeth—what had they ripped and torn at? Something alive, no doubt—something alive but dying.

What time do you got Bruce?

Bruce looked at the watch his Father had got him for Christmas last year.

A man should have a good watch, had said Father.

The face looked up at him.

It's about three, said Bruce. He swung his stick.

Don't hit me with that, snapped Earl. Be careful—

I am.

He palmed the dome of the cat skull in his pocket and the face looked out into the dark of his pocket from between his fingers, but saw nothing because the eyes were empty. Earl's forefinger picked at a bit of flesh stuck to the skull below the eye—dry leathery flesh tufted with fur. He picked a bit free and it fell into the darkness of the bottom of the pocket where all the lint and dirt and scraps of torn paper and filthy pocket change was. His other hand flexed in the empty pocket— jealous in a way of the other. It felt cold and clammy. It was deep autumn. Bare trees passed by grasping. Golden leaves lay in the dunes. The air; cold.

It's a lousy time of the year, said Earl. It's so cold and gloomy—

Ah I don't mind it, muttered Bruce. Christmas is coming—

Christmas with the live Christmas tree that the tabby cat would sniff around paw at and chew on, thought Earl. His forefinger was in the nose of the cat face. The jaw moved a little; but remained attached held by the dried remnants of the tendons of the face.

Yeah, said Earl. Christmas—

His words trailed off as a gist of chilly wind gripped up a bunch of leaves into a whirl out in the dunes. The cat eyes pressed into his palm. If there had been eyes there, they would not have been able to see anyway. No live cat would stand for this; it would writhe and twist and claw its way away; they had almost reached Washington Avenue, where they would leave the tracks and turn right toward home. Tract houses would pass them; one after the other after the other and on. They left the tracks and began that way. Bruce dragged the stick along the sidewalk. They walked between the mailboxes and the driveways and the all the same houses. Earl pressed one cat eye with his palm; just one, now. But the other could still not see, anyway. It wasn't the dark of the pocket; it was the dead of the cat.

From the Ides of March to Mayday 2012

On wheels and on foot,
The family tree expands its borders
In the four directions of delight,
Finding refuge from winter
In sun dappled shadow,
Finding respite from summer
On twilight verandas,
Where viewers tweet secrets and
Contestants sing praises
To the pastas of spring
Gnoshing with fishes,
Faceless and nameless,
On the Lower East Side.

Living small is the best revenge,
Analyzing the couch
In a just so apartment
With friends in a
World of one's own
Might be tiny but thrilling,
Healing an act of defiance,
And owning the past
A declaration of freedom.

Lessons in the history
Of the hard sell
Abound rebound
And reverberate
With songs of lament
In the mind of a con man
For the vicious end
Of a battered fortune,
Where the American

Dream explodes
Into clutch of cactus flowers
Along a lonely desert track
Dreaming of the next rain.

Swimming

I inhaled gasoline fumes. I was ten. I have no idea how I knew that breathing vapors would get you high, your mind thick, silly, forgetting. Sneaking along the nighttime edges of 1960s starter homes lined up on stark Bermuda lawns, I would feel for the greasy, metal surfaces of push mowers in sheds, unscrew the caps and breathe.

~~~

Insider's joke: The trapeze artist grips the bar in his mouth over empty space, no net. Alcoholics let go on purpose. They drop willingly into forgetting oblivion.

~~~

I don't remember my first meeting.

But I recall sitting with a pudgy, sixty-something woman in cotton jeans at a diner afterwards.

Diners look the same on the outside: sticky booths, griddle cooks, single patrons eating, smoking, staring off into memories. Ellie and I hunched over stained Formica, drinking coffee and pushing stale apple pie around on our plates. We looked like a grandmother and her twenty-two-year-old granddaughter.

"I missed a dance routine at a national competition. I was passed out in my hotel room in my tutu."

"That's alcoholism."

"I stole cheap wine from the A & P behind my parents' house."

"That's alcoholism."

"Lost jobs. Quit high school. Kicked out of bars. Relationships sucked dry."

"That's alcoholism."

"When I was fifteen, a friend I drank with committed suicide. She got her dad's gun. Shot herself in the park beside her house, her mother probably sewing or baking. Oblivious."

"Do you feel suicidal?"

"No," I chuckled. "I don't have that much courage."

~~~

Bridges attract suicides. Most people die from the trauma of impact. They free fall for several seconds into the blue oblivion before their bodies collide with the water at approximately seventy-five miles per hour. The coroner can approximate the angle at which the body hits the water by the injuries. A few jumpers outlive the drop. They usually die from hypothermia or drowning.

~~~

I remember this much about my second meeting.

The breakout groups had gathered for the closing. People sat in cockeyed rows of folding chairs and leaned against dusty walls. They stood in the doorway and spilled out into the basement hallway of the church which had donated space to help them remember. Most were sober. Some were not—able to face their memories. Crumpled one-dollar bills and loose change filled a basket like you might put candy in for trick-or-treaters. Cigarette smoke escaped through the opened transom windows which were supposed to let in the September air, hot and close even at 9:00 p.m.

Ellie rubbed my back.

Missy held a tray of plastic poker chips and passed each token in front of her like the Eucharist.

I pushed my chair back to give my legs room.

I understand what Stevie Smith means by "not waving, but drowning."

In the sixth grade, I got knee-collapsing sloshed in my neighbor's darkened living room, a pair of scissors in one hand, a bottle of Boone's Farm in the other—a short cut or long cut to forgiving oblivion. The television screen waves of white noise.

~~~

"Are you alright?" Ellie asked.

I jumped.

"Oh, yes. I'm fine. Thank you." I could be a polite drunk, like the southern debutante I never was getting tipsy from her first chilled mimosa on the veranda. Or fouled mouthed, I could scream at my horrified mother, "Kiss my ass," when she threatened my air supply.

143

"We have the white chip for anyone who would like to give up the high cost of low living and join us," Missy said.

On dry land, some addicts laughed easily, confession, indeed, good for the soul. Others clung to any flotsam floating by, their smiles guarding their secrets and their bottles.

I inhaled and held my breath.

"Would anyone like a white chip?"

Adrenaline rushed up my legs.

~~~

An alcoholic by eighteen, I went with my mother to a church camp with seventy-five-mile mountain views. I stayed high that weekend on the living water of Christ. On Sunday morning, perched on a rock outcrop, I floated on the blue horizon. I drank for four more years, but mom and I would attend country revivals, altar calls drawing me down the red-carpeted aisles, strangers praying "hallelujah."

~~~

I don't remember when I learned to swim. But by ten years old, I swam a solid backstroke. I could dive—sleek and long—off the starter's block, hold my breath and paddle my feet in mermaid waves, pushing my body farther and farther before breaking the surface.

Winter Walk
Chicken Ranch Beach, Inverness

My shadow stretches
into a long cloud, follows me,
settles into the sand with each step,
slithers around stones
in a mischievous way.
For a time we amble together
in peace along the bay.

But today sudden change,
oblique light descends,
sculpts swiftly moving clouds.
Heavy skies hug chilled air,
a surrender to winter's
rebellious ways.

As balance quivers
in uncertainty, crows
hatch a scavenger's plan.
Tall pines huddle
in a pool of blackness.
Their ragged edges etch the sky.
Branches shiver, waters
tremble onshore.

No shadow to follow me home
as I enter this season of mulling,
shaded lamps, fireplace nights.
A time for swift walks
warmed by my inner light.

AUTHORS

Erik Bendix
Erik Bendix's poetry distills silence of the woods he lives in, joy in music and poignancy of his family's Holocaust survival. A student of movement arts from Tai Chi to dervish whirling, he listens for how cadence resonates in the body. He has translated Rilke's complete "Duino Elegies" and "Sonnets to Orpheus." His work has appeared in the *Asheville Poetry Review, Monarch Review, Word Riot, St. Anne's Review, Forge, Poetry East* and *Euphony*.

Randall Brown
Randall Brown teaches at Rosemont College's MFA in Creative Writing Program. He is the author of the award-winning collection "Mad to Live" (*Flume Press*, 2008), his essay on (very) short fiction appears in *The Rose Metal Press* "Field Guide to Writing Flash Fiction: Tips from Editors, Teachers, and Writers in the Field, and he appears in the Norton Anthology of Hint Fiction" (*W.W. Norton*, 2010). He blogs regularly at FlashFiction.Net and has been published widely, both online and in print, including online at *American Short Fiction, Tin House,* and *Mississippi Review*, and in-print in *Cream City Review, Lake Effect,* and *Harpur Palate*.

Caroline Bruckner
Caroline attended the National School of Film and Television in London and got an MA in screenwriting. Her film, "The Confession," won a student Oscar in 2010 and was nominated for an Academy Award in 2011. Also, an animated film Caroline wrote, "Cooked," was selected for the Cinéfondation in Cannes Film Festival in 2010. Her short fiction has been featured in *Diverse Voices Quarterly* and *Willow Review*.

Gladys Justin Carr

Gladys Justin Carr is a recovering corporate executive now writing full time. Formerly Publisher & VP at *Harper Collins* book publishers, she is the author of a poetry chapbook, "Augustine's Brain--The Remix," and co-author of "Edge by Edge." Her recent work has appeared in over 90 literary magazines nationwide and in Canada. She is a winner of a *California State Poetry Society Award* and has been nominated 3 times for the *Pushcart Prize*. She is listed in "Who's Who in America" and "Who's Who in the World," probably because she is an internationally renowned chocoholic.

Daniel Clausen

Daniel Clausen has veins that circulate 1930s pulp fiction. When he bleeds Philip Marlowe appears. His work has been published in *Slipstream Magazine, Leading Edge Science Fiction,* and *Black Petals.* His new book is "The Ghosts of Nagasaki."

Douglas Collura

Douglas Collura is the author of the book, "Things I Can Fit My Whole Head Into," which was a finalist for the 2007 *Paterson Poetry Prize.* He was also the 2008 First Prize Winner of the *Missouri Review Audio/Video Competition in Poetry.* His work has been published in *The Alembic, BLACK&WHITE, The Broome Review, Coe Review, The Cynic, Dislocate, The Dos Passos Review, Eclipse, The Evansville Review, Forge, Paterson Literary Review, Lips Magazine, Many Mountains Moving, The Monarch Review, Sanskrit Literary-Arts Magazine, Sierra Nevada College Review, Salt Hill Journal, Soundings East, Spillway, Stickman Review, 2Bridges Review,* and other periodicals and webzines.

Patrick Curley

Patrick Karl Curley is a poet and playwright from the north west of Ireland. Previous dramatic works include "Beneath The Bone Moon", and a theatrical adaptation of Dostoyevsky's "Crime and Punishment."

Arthur Davis

Arthur Davis is a management consultant, has been quoted in *The New York Times, Crain's New York Business*, interviewed on New York TV News Channel 1, taught at the New School University, given testimony as an expert on best practices for the U.S. Senate and appeared as an expert witness on best practices before The New York State Commission on Corruption in Boxing. He has written 11 novels and over 130 short stories. Over 40 stories have been published online and in print.

Jeffrey Dieter

Jeffrey Dieter began writing poetry at a young age as a way to cope with the sudden, violent death of his father. For him, writing poetry was cathartic and a means of escape. Jeffrey expanded his writing abilities beyond the confessional/personal by attending Goucher College in Towson, Maryland, and studying with the poet Elizabeth Spires. He currently lives in Baltimore, Maryland.

George Dila

George Dila's short story collection "Nothing More to Tell" was published by *Mayapple Press* in 2011. His short fiction chapbook "Working Stiffs: three stories about work" is forthcoming from *One Wet Shoe Press* in Spring 2014. George's personal essays and short stories have appeared in numerous journals, and earned several awards and prizes. A native Detroiter, George now lives and writes in the small Lake Michigan shore town of Ludington.

Willem Donahue

Willem is an existential wreck from Connecticut. He is an American mystic and a lazy writer. He calls this the golden age of poetry because nobody's reading it. He was published once in a magazine called *Chronogram*.

Michael Emery

Michael grew up in the Lost River Valley of east/central Idaho—cow country, the last of the Old West; he left knowing all he needed to about cows, coyotes, fences, rattlesnakes, fly fishing, hunting, and drinking beer, but not much about the background basics for a modicum of learning. As an undergrad at Occidental College, Michael worked a variety of odd jobs to finance my degree in psychology and philosophy. From there, he attended the Teachers College at Columbia University for his Ph.D. in clinical psychology. Eric went on to spend some time in the Peace Corps before returning to Idaho, quitting psychology, and buying a ranch. His decision to return to professional practice led him to work for the court system as a forensic psychologist, handling competency, child custody, personal injury, and criminal sentencing issues. Now semi-retired, Eric came to New Mexico via the Creativity and Madness continuing education series and now live at an artist's colony in El Morro. His writing has been published in *Grey Sparrow Journal, Schuylkill Valley Journal,* and "The Zuni Mountain Poets: An Anthology," edited by John Carter-North, Margaret Gross, and Thomas Davis.

Joseph Farley

Joseph Farley edited *Axe Factory* from 1986 to 2010. His books and chapbooks include "Suckers," "For the Birds," "Longing for the Mother Tongue," "Waltz of the Meatballs," "Her Eyes," and "Crow of Night." His work has appeared recently in *Danse Macabre, Concrete Meat Sheets, Thunder Sandwich, Horror Sleaze Trash, US 1 Worksheets, Verse Wisconsion, Visions and Voices, Whole Beast Rag,* and other places.

Mike Finley

Mike Finley is coauthor with master bread baker Danny Klecko in three 2013 chapbooks: "Out For a Lark," "The Bluebeard of Happiness," and "A Pox Upon Your Blessings." In his spare time Mike runs *Robots & Pirates,* a Twin Cities organization helping punks in trouble.

Pamela Hammond

Pamela Hammond was born in Chicago, grew up in Southern California, and now lives in Santa Monica. She earned a bachelor's degree from UCLA and a master's degree from California State University, Northridge. She worked for a start-up visual art magazine in Los Angeles, images and issues, and then developed her own periodical, *Eye International*. She became a Los Angeles-based critic for Art News based in New York, reviewing exhibitions for more than a decade. Her love of nature has led her to hike, backpack, and travel, often to Northern California, and to Alaska, the Southwest, Hawaii, and New Zealand's South Island, which became her home for almost a year. She completed two chapbooks, "Encounters" (2011) and "Clearing" (2012), produced by *Red Berry Editions*, Fairfax, California. In 2013, her work appeared in *Forge, Assisi, Foliate Oak, Broad River Review*, and *Tulane Review*. In 2014, her work will appear in *Whistling Shade*.

Michael Haskins

Michael Haskins is an M.F.A. candidate in fiction at Oklahoma State University.

Mureall Hébert

Mureall Hébert lives in the Pacific Northwest with her husband and three kids. Her work has appeared or is forthcoming in a variety of print and online magazines, including *Suddenly Lost in Words, Stone Crowns Magazine, Bartleby Snopes,* and *Short, Fast, and Deadly*, among others. She's an MFA graduate from the Northwest Institute of Literary Arts.

Alyssa Hubbard

Alyssa Hubbard is author to "Humans and Their Creations," "An Austrian March," and the Apocalyptia series. Her poetry has been featured in *Crack the Spine* and *scissors & spackle*. She is currently attending the University of Alabama for a BA in English with a minor in Creative Writing. She loves blogging and singing in public.

151

Rosabelle Illes

Rosabelle Illes (26), is an Aruban artist. She is the author of two collections of poetry and the creator of an art calendar. Her short story "Stars for sale: a buck each" (2013), about a woman who becomes mentally ill as a result of countless coffee cups bearing her misspelled name, is published in *Gone Lawn Journal's* 11th issue. Her experimental piece "The invisible short story" (2013) features in the *NewerYork Press*. Presently, she is working on a children's book in collaboration with singer songwriter Levi Silvanie. She holds a BA in Psychology (Hons) and a minor in English Literature from Webster University and an MSC. in Social and Organizational Psychology from Leiden University, where she is currently a doctoral candidate.

Romana Iorga

Romana Iorga is a Romanian-American writer living in Virginia. She has published two previous collections of poetry in her native language. In the US, her work has also appeared in *2RiverView, Radical Society, Fickle Muses, Dislocate, Crab Creek Review, Maverick Magazine,* and others.

Vicki Iorio

Vicki Iorio's poetry has appeared in *The San Pedro Review, Spillway, 'hell strung and crooked', Tattoosday, Reckless Writing* as well as other print and online publications. "Poems from the Dirty Couch," Iorio's first full length poetry collection was published in the spring of 2013. Vicki Iorio, a native Long Islander, believes poetry saved her life more than once.

Kimberly Lojewski

Kimberly Lojewski writes and teaches at UMass Amherst. She has been published in *PANK, Gargoyle, Drunken Boat, Jersey Devil Press, Burrow Press,* and elsewhere. She is currently finishing a book of short stories and a new nonfiction project.

Angela Consolo Mankiewicz

Angela Consolo Mankiewicz has published 4 chapbooks, the most recent are "An Eye," published by *Pecan Grove Press* and "As If," from *Little Red Books-Lummox*. Publications include: *Poets/Artists, Full of Crow, Long Poem Magazine* (UK), *Poiesis, PRESA, Montserrat, Re)Verb, BrooklynVoice, Seldom Nocturne, Istanbul Literary Review, Arsenic Lobster, Temple/Tsunami, Slipstream, Chiron Review, Hawaii Review, Cerberus, Karamu, Lynx Eye, Pemmican, ArtWord*. Other recognitions include 2 *Pushcart* nominations and 1st and Grand Prizes from *Trellis Magazine, JerseyWorks,* and *Amelia*. She has also been the Contributing Editor and Regional Editor, respectively, for the small (now defunct) journals *Mushroom Dreams* and *The New Press Quarterly* and is a regular contributor for *Small Press Review*. Last May, her chamber opera, "One Day Less," music by D. Javelosa, was performed at the Broad 2nd Space in Santa Monica, CA.

Kathleen McCormick

Kathleen McCormick's work has been widely published in such journals as *CAYLX, Northwest Review, Paterson Literary Review, PMS poemmemoirstory, The Rambler, A River and Sound Review, South Carolina Review, Superstition Review,* and *Witness,* among others. Her full-length memoir, *Riding Downhill with No Hands,* on growing up in Cambridge, Massachusetts, in the '60s and '70s as an Italian-Irish Catholic girl with a vivid imagination and a confused sense of selfhood, is currently in circulation. In 2009, Kathleen's piece, "I Always Felt Like I Was On Good Terms With The Virgin Mary, Even Though I Hadn't Gotten Pregnant In High School," was awarded first prize for a personal essay by *Tiny Lights,* and a staged reading of it was performed in California in the summer of 2012. She is currently negotiating with a New York-based theater company to adapt her personal essay "Practice Boyfriend" for the stage. Kathleen is a professor of literature and writing at Purchase College, State University of New York, and has written/edited seven academic books, including *The Culture of Reading and the Teaching of English* (Manchester UP and St. Martin's, 1994), which won the MLA's Mina Shaughnessy Award.

Jeni McFarland
Jeni McFarland is an MFA in Fiction at the University of Houston. She is a Michigander, and has worked previously on a snow removal team for a roofing company, as a housekeeper for a hotel, and as the pastry chef of a country club. Her writing has appeared in *Spry, Forge,* and elsewhere.

Jim Meirose
Jim Meirose's work has appeared in numerous magazines and journals, including *Collier's Magazine, the Fiddlehead, Witness, Alaska Quarterly review,* and *Xavier Review,* and has been nominated for several awards. Two collections of his short work have been published and his novels, "Claire","Monkey", and "Freddie Mason's Wake" are available from Amazon.

Tania Moore
Tania Moore's stories have appeared in *About Place Journal; A Retrospective of the Civil Rights Movement, Quiddity, Kestrel, The Other Journal; an intersection of Culture and Faith, Opium, Sheepshead Review* and many others. She was a semi-finalist for the 2013 *William Van Dyke Short Story Prize* and a finalist for the 2012 *bosque Fiction Award,* and has been anthologized in *Up, Do, Flash Fiction.* Having earned her MFA from Columbia University School of the Arts, where she was the recipient of the *C. Woolrich Fellowship* for fiction, Tania teaches creative writing in New York area schools and lives and works along the mighty Hudson River.

Peter Obourn
Peter's work is forthcoming or has appeared in *Bombay Gin, CQ (California Quarterly), descant, Forge, Gastronomica, Inkwell, Kestrel, The Legendary, Limestone, The Madison Review, New Orleans Review, North*

Atlantic Review, North Dakota Quarterly, Oyez Review, PANK, Quiddity Literary Journal, Red Wheelbarrow Literary Magazine, SNReview, Spillway, Stickman Review, Switchback, Viral Cat, Wild Violet, The Write Room, and The *Blueline Anthology 2004.* Peter's short story, "Morgan the Plumber," which appeared in *North Dakota Quarterly,* has been nominated for a *Pushcart Prize.*

Val Dering Rojas

Val Dering Rojas is a Los Angeles based poet and artist. Her poetry and short fiction has been included in *Referential Magazine, Dogzplot, ken*again,* and *Right Hand Pointing* among others. Her chapbook, "Ten," is available from *Dancing Girl Press.*

Helen Sinoradzki

Helen Sinoradzki has completed a memoir, "Thursday's Child," about the eight years she spent in a Catholic cult. She writes fiction and narrative nonfiction and has published both in various on-line journals. Helen is a former English teacher turned technical writer and then bookseller. Her current day job is selling books at Powell's Books in Portland, Oregon, where she lives with her husband. She attends *Pinewood Table,* a weekly writing group led by Stevan Allred and Joanna Rose.

Malissa Stark

Malissa Stark, a Colorado writer, is honored to be published in *Crack the Spine.* Her work has also been featured in *The Story Week Reader, Friction,* and her nonfiction in *The Chicago Tribune.* When not writing she enjoys biking, hiking, and anything outdoors.

Pierrette Roleau Stukes

Pierrette Rouleau Stukes has published creative nonfiction on *The Dead Mule School of Southern Literature,* in *Mountain Memoirs: An Ashe County Anthology,* in *The Rose, on Crack the Spine,* and on *The Big Roundtable.* Her essay "Swimming" was awarded first place in a regional creative nonfiction contest. "Tilted Toward Life" was nominated for the 2011 Best of the Net for nonfiction. A short-short fiction story, "Between the Lines," earned an Honorable Mention in *New Millennium Writings*. Her nonfiction memoir essay "Misinformation Effect" has also earned an Honorable Mention in *New Millennium Writings*.

This anthology is generously sponsored by Outskirts Press

anything

everything

everywhere

WITH

"It just doesn't get any better than this."
—Deanna O'Leary,
    published Outskirts Press author

 Writing Services to help you start, finish, or edit a book.

 Publishing Packages to help you publish and distribute.

 Marketing Support to help you promote your book.

Visit www.outskirtspress.com for 10% off a publishing package with promotion code: CTS2013

157

Visit www.crackthespine.com to subscribe to our weekly digital magazine or to review our submission guidelines.

www.ingramcontent.com/pod-product-compliance
Lightning Source LLC
Chambersburg PA
CBHW070550180626
46817CB00005B/1770